Climbing Towards Excellence
how to get the best for students at GCSE

Unive
Subje

ht

Climbing Towards Excellence
how to get the best for students at GCSE

John R Rowling and Wyll Willis

Trentham Books

Stoke on Trent, UK and Sterling, USA

Trentham Books Limited
Westview House   22883 Quicksilver Drive
734 London Road   Sterling
Oakhill   VA 20166-2012
Stoke on Trent   USA
Staffordshire
England ST4 5NP

First published 2006

British Library Cataloguing-in-Publication Data
A catalogue record for this book is available from the British
Library

ISBN-13: 978-1-85856-383-1
ISBN-10: 1-85856-383-6

Cartoons:
pages 4, 54, 70 © by kind permission of Arnold Fletcher
page 35 © *The New Yorker* Collection 1983 Sam Gross from
cartoonbank.com All Rights Reserved
page 46 © *The New Yorker* Collection 2000 Alex Gregory from
cartoonbank.com All Rights Reserved
page 108 © *The New Yorker* Collection 1984 Bruce Eric Kaplan
from cartoonbank.com All Rights Reserved

Designed and typeset by Trentham Print Design Ltd, Chester and
printed in Great Britain by Bemrose Shafron (Printers) Ltd,
Chester

What senior staff who have used the principles and practices in this book say about it

■ *Thought provoking, stimulating and necessary reading for all school leaders.* Andreas Andreaou, deputy head, Virgo Fidelis College, Croydon

■ *Fantastic yet easy to grasp ideas. Makes me wonder why we haven't thought of them before! Helps you get away from the can't do restrictions of the standard Key Stage 4 curriculum to so that's what we can do. I recommend it to all aspiring school leaders.* Bec Allott, headteacher, Cheam High School, Sutton

■ *An absolute gripper! I just could not put it down, made me late for period 5 on a Friday afternoon* Andy Lazarevic, Assistant headteacher, Swakeleys School, Hillingdon

■ *When considering whether to go to a meeting I always wonder first about whether I will bring back something useful for the school. Often the value of training or conferences is in the unstructured time talking to colleagues when an idea strikes a chord: Tim Brighouse calls these ideas butterflies. Having been to meetings where the ideas in this book were shared over the course of a year I am sure you will find some exotic and colourful species within its pages. Not all of them will fit your school but I'm pretty sure that something here will find a new home with you.* Colin McKinlay, headteacher, Coulsdon High School, Croydon

■ *Motivation improved markedly when we used some of the ideas in this book. Creating a competitive revision system had significant impact. I would recommend these ideas to anyone trying to improve examination results.* Chris Pendlebury, deputy head, Emerson Park School, Havering

■ *This is an outstanding book, full of great ideas to help a school reach its targets. Every senior school leader should read it.* Barbara Rhymaun, headteacher, Darrick Wood School, Bromley

■ *Anybody who is in the business of motivating should read this! Practical ideas that work to motivate the motivator.* Chris Lamb, deputy headteacher, Bishop Douglass RC School, Barnet

■ *The ideas in this book made a fantastic impact on both students and staff involved in our raising achievement programme. They inspired, motivated and raised the self esteem of students to a higher level.'* Mark Conroy, raising achievement leader, Hendon School, London

■ *This book is a must for anybody who is serious about improving the life chances of their students. Our GCSE results improved by 14% in the first year. The authors deliver the message in the book with real passion and commitment. Importantly, the advice does work.* Nick Ware, headteacher, The Priory School, Orpington

■ *Eston Park School had access to these ideas over a number of years. The practical insights and suggestions helped us to fine tune our practice and maximise the strengths, skills and dynamism of our staff.* Jim Rogers, headteacher, Eston Park School, Middlesbrough

■ *For all those leadership teams seeking ways of motivating staff and students to aspire to high achievement this book is essential reading. Strategies are rooted in an excellent value system and have been tried and tested by committed professionals.* Jenny Vickers, Director of Professional Development, City of York

Contents

Writing about climbing is boring. I would rather go and climb. Chuck Pratt

Acknowledgements

Dale Carnegie wrote people rarely succeed unless they have fun in what they are doing. We know that on this journey you never reach the top but we want you all to know you make the journey fun.

We don't much like the word acknowledgements. You acknowledge that you have a headache but you are not pleased about it. These acknowledgments are more about appreciation. When you begin to climb towards excellence you need support, encouragement, commitment, enthusiasm, comradeship and envisioning. These people have provided some or all of those things for us:

All the headteachers and senior leaders of the partnership in London schools who have been open to listen, learn and share and have become friends as well as colleagues.

Barbara, Geraldine, Colin, Nick, Richard, Sister Bernadette, Jenny, Geoff, Angela, Carol, Meryl, David, Christian, Sue, Andy, Mark, Lauren, Christine, Viv, Veronica, John, Bec, Stephen, David, Gerry, Peter, Dave, Rhianne and Carol: thank you for letting me into your schools and touch things that are precious to you.

Anna and Hannah, colleagues at the Department for Education and Skills who have worked alongside us so supportively for two years to help us climb towards excellence

Jenny, your encouragement and support are appreciated a great deal

Michael Fullan whose ideas stimulated so much in us and gave us the conviction that our impulses and instincts were well-grounded and provided the impetus to get moving

The teachers who have been in teams with us for different parts of our journey and left a deep and lasting impression: Stephen, Dee, David, Andrew, Kathy, Barry and so many more

Sheila, Rachel, Nick and Sarah; appreciated more than words can say

John Watt with your quiet strength and ability to fritter

David Evans whose personal and professional companionship has been invaluable

David Hudson gave the opportunity to make a difference in Rotherham and the opportunity to work alongside the Pridster and Chris: so much has been learned from you

Richard, Mike and Terry have such joy and passion for teaching at the end of their careers and Lauren and Katie who begin theirs with such a commitment to influence young people, provide inspiration and create humility

The Blackwood Six who remind us there is a world outside teaching and for making it so much fun

Andy and Hermione for your ideas and support

Jonesy who remains the most interesting and wonderful person I have ever met: your love underpins everything I am. Sam and Em we are both so proud of you

Our students, with the passing of the years, too many to mention. You are the reason why we do what we do. Your happiness and success is our reason for being.

Gillian, you are a brilliant editor with remarkable skill.

Arnold Fletcher worked alongside the authors in their quest for excellence at Nunthorpe School and later joined Wyll at Wickersley High School, Rotherham. He has a deep understanding of his subject allied to a love of teaching. His huge intellect, acute perception and wicked humour made him an obvious choice to supply some cartoons. We are indebted to him.

Introduction

When I retired after 19 years of headship I did not expect to be involved in education quite as much as I had been. An invitation from the Department of Education and Skills to work on raising standards in some London Schools changed all that. It was a challenge I found irresistible. I knew little about the 22 schools I was invited to work with and they knew nothing about me. Our first meeting was tense and filled with suspicion – *Who is this man who is going to tell us where we have gone wrong?*

As it turned out, the tension and suspicion changed to friendship and agreement. I discovered headteachers keen to move forward, just as committed to excellence as I was. Most had programmes operating in school to raise standards, like mentoring and monitoring, but all found something new from our meetings together. Some said they had tried everything they could think of and were becoming frustrated at appearing to have reached a plateau. The early suspicion they experienced derived from the fear that here was another attempt to sit in judgement on them. What they discovered was a collaborative attempt to discover new ideas to impact on fulfilling student potential.

I accepted the challenge because I really believed that my time at Nunthorpe had given me an understanding of the underlying issues related to achievement at GCSE and a series of practical ideas that were transferable to other schools. I knew how much success would mean to colleagues in other places if it could be achieved and was eager to get going.

To its great credit the Department of Education and Skills through the London Challenge allowed me to use my own approach without interference. I will always be grateful for such trust.

It did not take long for the atmosphere in our meetings to change. Headteachers discovered that many of the principles and ideas were new and because they were supported by sound educational and psychological theory many began to introduce programmes based on them. These plans, working alongside some well-established good practice already going on, produced significant improvement in performance. In 18 of the schools working in this Collaborative initiative results were the best the school had achieved over the past five years. The results in two schools went up by over 14 per cent in a year.

This did not surprise me because it was clear that I was working with some very good and shrewd headteachers who were wide open to new ideas, ready to appraise their value and applicability and determined to implement measures to create success. I am full of admiration for them. They deserve the success they had. But I had seen this same transformation before. I knew that these ideas worked because I had seen them operating in other schools sometimes transforming performance by as much as 20 per cent in one year.

Wyll Willis is a long-standing friend and colleague. He had been a leader in Nunthorpe School on programmes to improve GCSE performance. When he was promoted, at the same time I left Nunthorpe, I was convinced he would make an impact on GCSE achievement wherever he went. And so it turned out. Using ideas outlined in this book alongside established good practice at Wickersley High School, results at GCSE went up by over 20 per cent in two years.

When we worked together we always insisted on explaining to those who came to see us to pick up *off the shelf solutions* to transform their GCSE performance that we were more interested in the process than the product. We emphasised the need to work out what we believed before we attempted to answer the question *what shall we do?* So it was we came to challenge our own practice about what motivates borderline students, what were the underlying issues associated with boys' underachievement and what were the purposes of trial examinations. Since those early days ever more sophisticated approaches have been taken and systems developed based on them. All these are outlined in this book.

Working with other headteachers so closely on such a practical and challenging issue as raising achievement at GCSE has been like a research project for me. I have discovered more and more ideas from them and as a result of talking with them have devised new ideas of my own which are being widely used by them and now by the additional 14 schools that are part of our Performance Collaborative in London. I am grateful for their insight and their willingness to explore ways to improve.

Both Wyll and I have been inspired by Michael Fullan. We first came across his work twelve years ago when he articulated the notion of moral purpose. Now this expression is widely used in educational circles but in those early days it rang bells with us. We were committed to making a difference and decided that we would insist that moral purpose should be explicit in planning initiatives about achievement. What we wanted to do had nothing to do with league tables but all to do with giving young people the best chance in life, opening up doors of opportunity and bringing them a sense of fulfilment, joy and pleasure.

It is with that in mind that we have joined together to write a book that will help you to do the same for your school.

John Rowling

Chapter 1

Why do we want to bring about change?

If we did all the things we are capable of doing we would literally astound ourselves
Thomas Edison

This book is for everyone who wants to see an improvement in their school's performance at GCSE in the 5 A* to C grades. It is not that these are the most important grades, simply that they are significant in the modern educational world. Having visited scores of schools, I know how hard many people are working to raise these examination grades but the big breakthrough just does not happen. Many people tell us they are doing everything they can think of. This book provides new ideas and fresh practical strategies that have proved effective. In the school where we first devised and tried some of these strategies results were raised from 59 per cent achieving 5A* to C up to 79.5 per cent over three years. Wyll moved to a school in 2003 where GCSE levels stood at 49 per cent. In two years this has risen to over 72 per cent. Where these ideas have been shared and implemented, allowing for some local adjustment, similar significant improvements have been made. Harrow High School achieved 33 per cent in summer 2004. In March 2005 it began to use the principles set out in this book, with brilliant application of ideas and commitment from a team of teachers and the headteacher, and results improved from 33 per cent to 47 per cent. Another school in Orpington, The Priory School, moved up by 12.4 per cent from 2004 to 2005. There are many more. They astounded themselves and so could you.

Standards cannot keep rising forever but there is substantial room for improvement in many schools. Many of the headteachers I have worked with have been ready to acknowledge that. And the first step is to realise that otherwise there is little chance of change. Michelangelo put it like this: *The greatest danger for most of us is not that our aim is too high and we miss it, but that our aim is too low and we reach it.* Aiming high and reaching the target has many benefits. Understanding these benefits will make you want to do something to raise standards for the students in your school.

You are a professional

At a meeting of headteachers of leading schools held in London, delegates asked each other why they thought they had been invited. It was suggested that they led very good schools and the hope was that they could share their practice with others. Modesty seemed to preclude some of them explaining what was particularly good about their school and what it was that made them excellent. It was either modesty or uncertainty. Sadly, if you don't know what it is that makes your school successful you are unlikely to be able to repeat it consistently. Too often I hear headteachers explaining success or failure in terms of a 'good year group' or a 'bad year group'.

I am amazed that we allow ourselves to believe that groups which have been under our influence for so long can simply be good or bad and implicitly unchangeable no matter what we have done. You are professional. You need to recognise the quality and the nature of any cohort of students early in their school lives and plan for success. This may involve additional resources to support more difficult groups, the financing of smaller classes or the deployment of strong pastoral staff. It certainly needs to be thought out and appropriate action taken. The professionalism of leaders makes them want to make the difference. It makes them want to devise ways of taking the raw material admitted to the school and bringing about transformation through clear, determined and decisive action. This is why headteachers and school leaders came into the profession. Yet excuses are common.

Jack Welch has a reputation as one of the great innovators of the past 75 years. In his book *Winning* (2005) he describes a typical board meeting where the subject is business improvement. He imagines everyone sitting around the table talking civilly about how hard it is to make significant improvements. They discuss the tough situation. They recite the same old reasons why they can't advance and why they are in fact doing well in their business. By the time they leave the meeting, they've managed to pat themselves on the back for the success they have achieved under the circumstances. And of course nothing changes. For board meeting read Senior Leadership Team: it's the same argument and the same excuses – with the same result. If you want to make significant improvement making excuses has to stop.

Ken Blanchard observed: *There is a difference between interest and commitment. When you're interested in something you do it only when it is convenient. When you're committed to something you accept no excuses only results.* The lead practitioners in schools are professionals but sometimes seem too ready to make excuses for the substandard

performance of students at GCSE. Common excuses include:

> 'It's a bad year group'
> 'There are far more boys in this year, what do you expect?'
> 'This lot don't want to work'
> 'This year group have suffered disruption through staffing problems'
> 'We get no support from parents'

The role and responsibility of the professionals is to plan to make the difference and allow no excuses. Not that these things are ever called excuses. They are presented as justifiable reasons or explanations, yet there are schools all over England achieving at a different and better level in much the same circumstances. Leaders in these schools want to make a difference and are absolutely committed because their professionalism demands it.

Professional leaders want to make a difference because they know how much better their staff would feel if they were able to do it. When staff realise their impact on the performance of students it generates enthusiasm, energy and momentum within the school so that success leads to success. It is much pleasanter to glory in success than seek explanations for failure. Just as a headteacher may not be able to explain what the school is doing to create success, teachers can sometimes not explain with clarity what they are doing to produce the results they achieve either. You want to raise standards and know how you did it so that staff can feel fulfilled and significant in their professional life.

You are aspirational

You want to do something to raise standards because you have high aspirations. Professional leaders know the impact of high standards on the reputation of the school in the community. It is nice not to fear comparisons with neighbouring schools because your results lag behind theirs, inviting disadvantageous comparisons by parents. And parents do make comparisons.

Teachers are not enthusiastic about League Tables but many parents are. They want to send their children to the school that offers them the best chance and often they judge that on the GCSE figures.

You are dissatisfied

In 1994 R Jacobs created an equation showing factors involved in creating successful change. It has applications everywhere in life.

$$P = A * B * D$$

where P is the probability that the change you want to make will succeed, A is dissatisfaction with the *status quo*, B is a clearly desirable end state and D is a series of specific steps on the way. The probability that you will be successful in raising the percentage of your students achieving five good GCSE grades will be proportional to the dissatisfaction you feel about the *status quo*. Many of the headteachers I have met have been quietly and internally dissatisfied with what is being achieved but are reluctant to talk about it openly for fear of creating demoralisation amongst staff. There is so much data available now that it is easy to see where the school stands against the expectations of others, whether these are held by Ofsted, the assessments shown in the Annual Data provided for schools or data from Fischer Family Trust.

Establishing the clearly desirable end state is not difficult either. Comparisons with similar schools or schools in your statistical family may begin the process by which you can visualise a desirable end position. When we were at 59 per cent this desirable end state for us would have been 65 per cent. Once you have this position established you are well on the way to devising strategies that can make it happen. Some of these strategies are outlined in detail in the following chapters.

You are under pressure

The introduction of League Tables has increased the pressure to achieve significantly. Perhaps that was the intention. Critics of these tables allege that this pressure has led to unscrupulous practice and an undue emphasis on what have become known as *borderliners*'. We called these students *key marginals*, a term stolen from the political world where the seats the party needs to get elected are so called. You might argue that getting elected is a selfish ambition, just as you might argue that a school is merely pursuing its own self-interest by focusing on key marginals. However, for every percentage point a school's results rise one or two students are achieving what they would not have achieved. The benefit is two-fold – both school and student are better off when each succeeds.

Even when professionals are happy with the *status quo* their masters often are not. Sometimes those masters are the DfES armed with its impressive statistical analysts' reports or the Governors, themselves under pressure from external inspection. The pressure is subtle but it is real. Increasingly salaries of headteachers and school leaders depend on success – now there's a pressure!

At a time when recruitment and retention of quality staff is not easy and the best teachers can choose their school, it doesn't help to produce results commonly known to be below expectations. A school that can point to improving standards is at an advantage in the recruitment process. Parents too are increasingly insistent on their choice of school. It is a pleasant and beneficial situation when there are queues of parents wanting their children to come to your school. The location of the school is of secondary importance to how it performs. Like it or not, this is most often judged by the performance of the key marginals; they are the ones that make the difference.

You enjoy making a difference

Tracey was newly appointed as headteacher of a Primary school in the North East of England. She had attended a conference where the issue of vision was discussed, particularly the importance of creating a picturesque vision. The summer before she took up her post, she came across the story of the small boy on the beach in America who was picking up starfish washed ashore by the tide. There were thousands of them – so many that an old man passing by told the boy, 'I wouldn't do that, you'll never make a difference. There are too many.' Picking up another and throwing it back into the sea, the boy replied, 'I will to that one.' Tracey decided she had found the right image for her vision. The starfish appeared in every classroom along with the slogan *Let's all make a difference to that one!*

Michael Fullan (2001) said Moral Purpose is about the drive to make a difference. Most school leaders have Moral Purpose in abundance and they do make a significant difference. It can extend to students' achievement too.

In 2002 we basked in the reflected glory of the outstanding achievements at our school. Three girls achieved 37 A* between them. Not bad! And two boys achieved nine and five A* to C grades. These were boys who had been in the bottom three percent when tested at age 11 and yet came out with results like that. We rejoiced with those splendid girls and gave them due praise but the hearts of the staff celebrated with those boys even more. They felt they had made a difference – and they had.

According to Alcoholics Anonymous *insanity is continuing the same behaviour and expecting a different result*. It is a slogan applicable to school too. When discussing the raising of achievement with a deputy headteacher recently, he admitted to feeling frustrated and discouraged. 'I have done everything I can think of,' he said, 'we want to improve but don't know what to do'. Remarkably honest; but unless we do try something new we are likely to keep getting the same results.

Creating significant change may demand the introduction of new ideas. If you keep doing what you've always done you'll keep getting what you always got. De Bono (2005) argues that

Arnold Fletcher

it is sometimes impossible for improvements to be made in the same direction. When young Fosbury invented the 'Fosbury flop' in the high jump, his intention was to keep his rear end from hitting the crossbar. This was such an improvement that the Fosbury flop has been the method of high-jumpers ever since. The older methods simply cannot compete. All improvement requires an element of change.

To qualify for creative change, a change can be small or big. You may need to consider big changes to achieve significant GCSE transformation.

Why do we want to raise the standards of achievement at Key Stage 4? All the reasons above and several more. But how do you do it? This book is written to share ideas to help you make it possible. It is not just a package of off-the-shelf ideas. Rather, it clarifies the rationale and principles that need to be understood before the hand reaches to the shelf. Nor is it a short term solution to a difficult issue. It is about fundamentals of practice that will influence the school far beyond the limited scope of Key Stage 4 results. However, it is particularly aimed at making a difference within a year and it is achievable. When you exceed the aspirational target, what joy it will bring. If you celebrate, so will we. We will feel that we too have made some difference.

Chapter 2

Bringing about change

Nearly everyone takes the limits of his own vision for the limits of the world. A few do not
Arthur Schopenhauer

Thank goodness for the few, those who break out of the confines of their limited thinking to do the remarkable. You do not have to be Christopher Columbus or Isaac Newton. Ordinary people also break out of their limitations to achieve what seemed impossible. Fosbury testifies to that. Clearly the impossible isn't.

■   It will be if you *believe* it is.

You won't even attempt the impossible if you are convinced it is unattainable. The boat will not leave the harbour if you have no belief that there is a distant shore. Once you do believe, it may take a while to persuade others to sail with you but without such belief you won't even try. Covey (2004) said: *All things are created twice: first, a mental creation; second, a physical creation.* These dreams or visions are not mere fantasies if they are based on a belief that change is possible.

■   It will be if you accept *current assumptions.*

The conclusion that something is impossible comes from accepting the assumptions in which your current practice is rooted. Your GCSE results will hardly vary from your present position if you accept your present assumptions about the ability of your students, the quality of your present systems or the appropriateness of your support structure. Have you assumed that present performance is the best your students can do? Have you assumed that the leadership of your academic subject leaders is drawing the best out of your students? Have you assumed that your motivational influence has reached its maximum potential? Have you assumed that boys will always perform less well than girls and always underachieve? Changing assumptions is difficult, mostly because they are never challenged; they are part of your life and contribute to your comfort zone. You can explain them coherently and with conviction. You have successfully convinced other influential people that this is how things are. Your world is flat so there is no thought of making a boat.

■   Impossible will remain impossible without *a change in thinking.*

Some of you are just beginning to think of a different world out there. You will need to. Einstein put it this way '*The significant problems we face cannot be solved at the same level of thinking we were at when we created them*'. Schools achieve what they do in large part because that is what they think they are capable of. Their performance is the outcome of the collective thoughts and efforts put into the standards' agenda. This is as true of outstanding performance as relatively poor results. It is possible that both outstanding and poor performance may be improved by a change in thinking about what is possible. In the latter case it is crucial.

■ The impossible will remain beyond reach if you are not *creative*.

At the time President Kennedy announced that America would put a man on the moon before the end of the decade, his scientific advisers gave him a barrage of reasons why that would be impossible. What he was promising simply could not be done. That should have been the end of the matter but Kennedy persisted, asking what the problems were. One reason was that no fuel existed that could do the job. Now he knew what the problem was Kennedy changed tack. 'It can't be done because the fuel does not exist. Then, if that is where we need to stretch, go create a fuel that will do the job.' And they did.

The problem was valid; no fuel did exist. However, the problem was not allowed to be the end of the debate. There will be real problems in your school that make the performance level what it is. Results stand at the level they are because no one has devised a *fuel* to move them into a different orbit. But it does not mean that such ideas do not exist, it means only that you have not thought of them yet. This book will help, as will new thinking by some staff in your school. The ideas are latent, simply not yet surfaced. Releasing creativity in your school is important. This may be stifled by *your* lack of creativity – not everyone is creative. That will only be a problem if you insist on holding everything close to your chest. The inventors of the new ideas may not be in the head's office or on the senior leadership corridor.

■ If you are *afraid to fail* the impossible is unlikely to happen.

Fear freezes endeavour, fear stifles new ideas, fear maintains the *status quo* or makes matters worse. Fear keeps you in the harbour instead of out on the seas, fear explains that things are not as bad as they are and any change will make matters worse. Fear magnifies the dangers inherent in change and drives you back to the safety of that which is known and understood. You will be tempted not to raise the standards question for fear of destabilising staff, of upsetting middle managers and awakening substantial opposition from vested interest groups. You will be tempted to draw back from asking challenging questions in case well-established heads of department express disquietude at best and outright opposition at worst. Best not stir up a hornets' nest. Fear points out how impossible the impossible really is!

Rene Carayol of Corporate Voodoo observed that

> *Organisations that have a reputation for changing the game, for achieving breakthroughs, have a restless energy about them that comes from the people who work in them. But ponderous, plodding organisations are afraid to allow their people free reign, practising a control culture that ensures that the energy in their people remains untapped.*

You can't make the impossible happen on your own but you can certainly stop it happening on your own. If you operate with a command and control culture you are not likely to see much creativity from the workforce. Sir Nick Scheele of Ford Motor Company had this view:

> *Leadership is about energising people. You need to turn the pyramid upside down. See yourself as the support service for your workforce. It takes some shift in context as a leader to be able to do this.*

Some schools have seen a dramatic shift in performance by allowing groups of younger staff to take some responsibility for raising standards from senior leadership where it rested for years. Ideas on how this might be done are explored later in this book.

■ Achieving the impossible requires a shift from *thinking incrementally*.

Some of the steps are incremental but the mindset and ambition is radical. Landing a man on the moon is not incremental. Talking with staff about making a one or two percentage point shift in GCSE performance is likely to be limiting. One or two per cent can be affected by the holiday plans of disengaged families. A headteacher I met recently bewailed the fact that two of his certainties for five or more GCSEs were going to Spain with their family on the day GCSE started. Despite phone calls and letters, off they went and with them 2 per cent of the GCSE results for that school. Many schools are more likely to achieve the impossible if they set a target that is not a small incremental shift. But has not to be a leap in the dark. Aiming for significant change is fine and admirable so long as it is accompanied by the implementation of a series of substantial ideas.

■ The impossible is more likely to be achieved by being *single-minded.*

People aiming to achieve excellence are naturally wired to focus on one thing at a time. Research indicates that if you have an 80 per cent chance of implementing an initiative with excellence, by adding a second initiative at the same time your chances of success slump to 64 per cent. Continuing to add initiatives until you have five operating simultaneously reduces your chances of success to 33 per cent. The impossible is more likely to be achieved by being *single-minded.* The sculptor Rodin created a wonderful, lifelike marble horse. When asked how he had created such an amazing likeness he commented

> *I found a large piece of marble, took a hammer and chisel and cut away everything that did not look like a horse.*

That is what single-mindedness does. Creating outstanding results is a work of art. It requires focus. It demands a place high on the agenda. It demands a team with little else in mind. There are so many conflicting demands for time and attention. Those who achieve excellence do so by cutting away everything that does not look like the standards they have set their heart on. Single-mindedness like that creates an outcome that people ask questions about.

■ The impossible will never happen unless you *take people with you*

Covey (2004) analysed the ways in which people choose to commit to a vision ranging from those whose action is to rebel or quit the team to those who engage with creative

excitement. The analysis showed these six behaviours:

■ rebel or quit
■ malicious obedience
■ willing compliance
■ cheerful cooperation
■ heartfelt commitment
■ creative excitement

Jo Owen (2005) says that selling an idea normally includes focusing on its *features*, its *benefits* and its associated *hopes and dreams.* The features of a project to raise standards are the actual rise you aim to achieve, alongside the processes you intend to adopt to bring it about. It will be best if the increase is specific and if the processes are clear and sufficiently detailed to sound convincing. The benefits will be presented as attractive and desirable and will be related to both the young people who achieve better results and the teachers who guide them. Most teachers want their students to do well and any practical steps that seem likely to bring that about find favour. You will have hopes and dreams and teachers do too. Getting them to share your hopes and dreams requires *pressing their hot buttons*; that is presenting the hopes and dreams in a way that gets them excited. Some teachers will engage with these ideas with spontaneity and enthusiasm and talk excitedly about little else for days. Often you can predict who these people will be because you will have seen this behaviour before. They are a vital asset and their enthusiasm needs to be used to the full. Others get to that stage eventually but are slower to ignite, sometimes more reflective and cautious. They start with willing compliance but can be encouraged and persuaded to move forward with the vision. It is essential not to chose as leaders those who are rebellious or maliciously obedient because they can be so destructive and kill an initiative before it has had chance to develop.

To achieve the impossible you need a team who have decided to engage with creative excitement. This does not happen by chance. It depends to some extent on how the vision of achieving the impossible is sold and how wise you are in selecting the leaders of it.

Chapter 3

Through vision

One day Alice came to a fork in the road and saw a Cheshire cat in a tree.

'Which road do I take?' she asked.

His response was a question: 'Where do you want to go?'

'I don't know,' Alice answered.

'Then,' said the cat, 'it doesn't matter.'

Lewis Carroll, *Alice in Wonderland*

Vision is about knowing where you want to go. As far as raising standards is concerned if you do not know where you want to be you are not likely to get there. Many schools I visit seem to operate on the same basis as I do with my golf: I know where I want the ball to go but I haven't much idea about how to get it there. Amazingly, sometimes it lands in the middle of the fairway but it is more by luck than skill and even if one shot manages to do that there is no guarantee the next one will. Still I know where I want the ball to go and that is the start.

If there is no appeal to excitement or self-interest people will be reluctant to embrace any vision. Burt Nanus (1992) talked of a

realistic, credible, attractive future for your organisation: an idea so energising that in effect it jump-starts the future by calling forth the skills, talents and resources to make it happen, and a signposting pointing the way for all who need to understand what the organisation is and where it intends to go.

That's some task. It will only be possible to create a vision like that if the leaders of the organisation are fully persuaded about it and feel it with some passion. You will not make it attractive to others if it is not attractive to you.

- Is shifting your GCSE performance by 10 per cent attractive to you?

- Can you imagine it happening? Is your dreaming realistic?

- Do you believe that your students could actually do that if the professionals got to work on it?

- Is this vision so clear and attractive to you that it jump-starts you?

Can you begin by thinking of two or three of your year 11 students who are believed to be unlikely to achieve 5 A* to C grades as things stand? Why not get their pictures, put them together in a happy group and add a slogan above the picture saying 'We'll make a difference to these three.' You don't show it to anybody – though that would probably confirm the intention in your mind. Simply keeping it in your drawer at home would be focus enough. Taking it one step further, you might create a local league table of examination performance in which your school appears considerably further up than before. Make it look as near to the real thing as possible except that this time you have shifted your school to where you would like it to be. Is that not attractive? Does that not spark a little self-interest alongside the deeper more important moral purpose? For two years our school had appeared in *The Times* annual list of top performing schools in England. The first year we were eighteenth in the list. Some of us imagined being in the top ten. It was a challenge. It was attractive, and it happened. The thinking about it, the imagining, propelled us into thoughtful action. The dreaming did not achieve the goal but it jump-started and intensified the efforts that did. Writing things down is important. Covey (2004) describes the process:

> *writing bridges the conscious and subconscious mind. It is a psycho-neuromuscular activity and literally imprints the brain.*

Canfield (2004) says *if you think it, ink it.* Anything that helps you focus on achieving the vision is worth serious consideration.

A goal is a dream with a date on it. Not a date somewhere so far away that people do not engage with it but sometime in the near future when the dream might be fulfilled. Nor should the dream be so vague and intangible that staff and students have no idea what you are aiming for. You will have no such difficulty if you determine a new figure for your GCSE performance one year from now. How to arrive at such a figure will be discussed in a subsequent chapter.

Rowling (2003) emphasised the need for creating a vision capable of being

imagined
achieved
adapted
talked about
desired
specified
understood
measured

Vision has to point to an outcome that most people want to happen, one they can imagine and that can be talked about easily. It has to be so specific that when it is achieved it is obvious. If the vision does not appeal to self-interest in the professionals they are not going to embark on the journey.

The vision for change in performance has to be launched with staff. It may be wisest to begin with a small group of staff you think are committed to the need for change. Collins (2001) argued that the best way to deal with issues like this is to *lead with questions not answers and to conduct autopsies without blame.* This reduces reluctance to engage in serious analysis. Understandably, teachers are reluctant to analyse if they fear they may be writing a suicide note if they do. Jack Welch believes that candour is lacking in many organisations. It is in many schools. He (2005) puts it like this:

> *Too many people don't express themselves frankly. They don't communicate straightforwardly or put forward ideas looking to stimulate debate. They just don't open up. Instead they withhold comments and criticism. They keep their mouths shut in order to make people feel better and avoid conflict, and they sugar coat bad news in order to maintain appearances. That's all lack of candour and it's absolutely damaging.*

You need some frank answers to questions like these:

> What should your students have achieved according to independent data analysts?
> What did they achieve? What is the difference? What are the brutal facts?
> What is the valued added statistic for the school between Key Stage 2 and Key Stage 4?
> What does your Local Authority believe about your performance?
> Which students did not achieve as highly as predicted?
> How many were there? What percentage of the year group did they represent?
> How many students achieved one, two,

three or four GCSE at C or better?

How well did you focus on them in year 11? Should they have achieved more?

What specific help did you provide for them?

What are other schools doing for students with the same prior attainment profile?

What systems do you have for finding out?

Which subjects are contributing to the school's success?

Which subjects are failing to add much to the school's success?

Which teachers are not achieving success? Do you know why?

What procedure do you have for holding subject leaders to account? Is it working?

Some uneasiness is inevitable but working through it will lead you to the view that standards can be changed. Sugar coating bad news is not helpful. Forming a group which will be open and honest might well discover some areas where improvement could be made.

Assuming you have sufficient support from that process and a surge in energy in those involved, you have a mandate to widen the statement of the vision to all staff in the school. A meeting of staff with a limited agenda is the most obvious launch pad for disclosing the vision. It is easy to add this vision to a full agenda and find it has been lost amongst a range of functional things. The big issue needs the big space. You may be sure it will take longer to make the vision clear than you had thought. Create the space for it so that by the end of the allocated time no one can be in any doubt what it is.

Leaders should consider carefully who communicates this vision. On the one hand, headteachers need to make it clear that they are wholly supportive of the vision. They may present it or they may prefer to invite some of the team of staff known to be engaged with the vision to make the presentations. It is often helpful if ideas are presented by members of staff, especially those with the ability to generate enthusiasm. Who presents the vision is less important than the need to ensure that the vision is clearly understood and attractive. The added advantage of a presentation by a member of staff is that their self-interest is nearer to that of other members of staff than that of senior leaders.

It is important that consideration is given to the cost of implementing the vision.

Don't ignore the cost

Jacobs (1994) argued that the probability of successful change is dependent on dissatisfaction with the *status quo*, the understanding of a clearly desirable end state and identifiable and specific steps on the way to that end. But Jacobs pointed out that the enterprise has to be worth more to staff than its cost. There is a cost involved for leaders. Embarking on an attempt to transform achievement will make huge demands on school leaders in terms of:

risk of failure

exposing underachievement for others to see and question

time and resources

leadership involvement in motivating and empowering teams of staff

more meetings with people

more accountability required from staff

constant vigilance on progress towards the goal over the course of one year

rooting out and dealing with issues that oppose the fulfilment of the vision.

It is easier not to get involved but there is a lot at stake. You know it is worth it and you believe you can do it but it is as well to calculate that there is a price to pay.

Don't underestimate the cost

Teachers have to pay a price too. This must not be ignored or underestimated. You may well be prepared to pay the price involved because you are perceived to have so much to gain. For them there is:

acknowledgement that they have fallen short of what could be achieved

thought to be given to being better at dealing with borderline students

- more personal accountability for how they handle these students
- public comparison with colleagues both in school and by parents at home
- a requirement for new action plans specifically designed to produce a better standard of exam performance.

Some will be reluctant to expose themselves to such scrutiny. They too have a comfort zone. Where there are new demands there should always be new support. Openly considering the cost produces disquiet but this can be mitigated by reassurance about the support offered. An equation attributed to Socrates links Empowerment of people with three issues, Autonomy (A), Direction (D) and Support (S).

$$E = A * D * S$$

Because you need all staff to contribute if standards are going to be raised, they need to be empowered to make their contribution. You will have to be sure that the autonomy they have and the directions they are given to raise standards is clear both in word and in action. They need confidence that they will not be left alone. They need your interest, your encouragement, generous resources and constant positive reward when they are giving evidence of wholehearted commitment.

Don't be deterred by the cost

It is plain that achieving the impossible is going to involve cost. As you become aware of the extent of it you may decide to retreat. I hope not. There is a lot at stake. Young people's hopes and futures are worth a great deal. Your own personal fulfilment will make it all worthwhile. You will be driven by those things to the point of full commitment. But your staff may not be so easily convinced. You will have to ensure that the goal is so attractive that it is worth the effort. You will have to describe what it is about this that appeals to their self-interest. You will have to say these things not once or twice but over and over again. Welch (2005) observed *there were times when I talked about the company's direction so many times in one day that I was completely sick of hearing myself.* You hear yourself saying the same things many times but others hear you a lot less. Care needs to be taken to repeat the vision again and again until you are sure it is embedded. Welch also advised that *to give any new venture a fighting chance you have to set it free. And you do need to spend more money on it and cheer louder and longer for it than may feel comfortable.*

The greatest problem with communication is the illusion that it has taken place. You will launch it clearly. You will want to create picture images of the vision to be displayed in the staffroom. You will need to repeat the vision consistently and regularly. You will report on the progress being made and tell the story of those who are successfully engaged with it. You will check that staff have heard and understood the vision. You will require departments and teams of people to consider aspects of the vision on a regular basis and to report back findings. You will provide opportunities for staff to ask questions and respond to them openly and fully. You will not allow the vision to diminish. You will speak constantly of the attractiveness of the intended outcome and reinforce the benefits and pleasures for staff in the future. You will not permit the vision to be hijacked by any issue no matter how significant. That way the impossible isn't.

Action points

- ■ Define what you want the GCSE performance to be
- ■ Plan a way to make this vision picturesque and unforgettable
- ■ Be clear and precise about the actions you intend to take
- ■ Prepare a launch with appropriate time allocated to it

Chapter 4

Through a designated team

Men wanted for hazardous journey. Small wages. Bitter cold. Long hours of complete darkness. Constant danger. Safe return doubtful. Honour and recognition in the event of success

Advert for recruits for Antarctic Expedition with Shackleton (1915)

It's amazing that with an ad like that anybody volunteered. But they did, no doubt attracted by the challenge and perhaps by the possibility of acknowledgement if they succeeded.

How can a leader move GCSE results up by 10 per cent? Can she do it herself? She could try but she is likely to fail. Leadership is not about doing all that needs doing, not even the matters of most significance. Leadership is about discovering ways to make the vision happen and employing suitable strategies to ensure that it does.

Can the Senior Leadership Team make it happen? Often this is the preferred model for schools. Delegating raising standards to a senior leadership team member is common. Deputy headteachers given this responsibility find it demanding and onerous. Several have told me it is one of their biggest areas of frustration. Landing such a responsibility on a deputy head is likely to have little success, for several reasons:

It is nearly always an *additional extra*. 'Could you take responsibility just this year because we need a senior member of staff to lead on this? Perhaps you can find time alongside all your other work.' Clearly there is no acknowledgement of the scale of the challenge or its importance. *No extra time* is given, leading to the interpretation that it will require little. If a deputy is to be used for this it will be as well to bear in mind Dean Fink's slogan (2003) 'always use 'instead of ' not 'as well as'.' Too often the raising standards agenda is 'as well as' other sizeable responsibilities. It does not work.

Apart from time, senior leaders have too *many distractions* to lead efforts to add 10 per cent to GCSE. They have a succession of meetings, making conflicting demands on any but the most organised person and relationships with students can often be distant and associated with discipline and sanctions. It is possible to combine all these aspects but it is not easy.

The inappropriateness of senior leaders heading an initiative like this is not meant to imply anything about their competence. Far from it. Without excellent leadership from the leaders no initiative in school will prosper. It is more that the role they fulfil is ill-suited to a major drive on raising standards unless it is a substantial, separate and significant part of their job and they are appointed to it because they have the qualities needed to make this challenge successful.

A hierarchical structure can stifle creativity. When all the big jobs are entrusted to senior leaders other people have little incentive to contribute ideas, energy and flair. Dourado and Blackburn (2005) reckon that *hierarchies value people for what they did yesterday. They imply that good ideas come from above.* Sometimes they do but not always, and in the case of driving up GCSE scores not often. PricewaterhouseCoopers conducted a study of non-creative organisations and observed that they have seven characteristics. They are

> prescriptive
> centralised
> risk averse
> hierarchical
> status conscious
> low level vertical communicators
> low level on trust.

These characteristics will kill initiative and will doom any attempt to push GCSE results significantly higher. A wider and wiser approach is needed, where possibilities are created by the leadership for others to be given an opportunity to fulfil their potential by engaging in a role with such huge implications. Welch (2005) called the vision the **big aha!** He reckoned that leaders *need to come up with a big aha for their school – a smart, realistic, relatively fast way to sustainable improvement.* Adding 10 per cent in a year qualifies as a big aha, don't you think?

But that was the first of Welch's significant steps to change. The second step was to *put the right people in the right jobs to drive the big aha forward.* Schools that have made this significant shift in performance have all created dynamic teams to drive the vision forward. Occasionally we have worked with schools who have not delegated it to a wider team. Almost invariably they have failed to hit the mark. Welch's final step was to *relentlessly seek out best practices to achieve your big aha, whether inside or outside your organisation, adapt and continually improve.* This book introduces some of the best practices being used at the moment. The secret is to take these ideas and others from wherever you can get them and to adapt and develop them. A team can do that.

What will a team member do?

A team is a group organised to work together to accomplish a set of objectives that cannot be achieved effectively by an individual. Team members are usually teachers in the school but support staff have been used successfully by some schools. When highly trained, given a clear remit and able to work with targeted students on intervention programmes, support staff make a valuable contribution to the standards agenda. The set of objectives in this team would lead to an increase of 10 per cent, say, on GCSE scores in your school.

Charged with responsibility for raising standards by 10 per cent or so, team members will need clear strategies to achieve such improvement. Practical proposals in this book include creating student teams to be judged on effort given to their work on a regular basis. Each team member will have five or six students to work with and will be responsible for developing improvements in their students' attitude and effort. They will meet the students weekly for motivational interaction, keeping records of the effort being made by the student. They will need to analyse progress, discuss with the student, recommend ideas to encourage change, monitor responses, check with staff on issues related to each student, encourage and reward progress being made, challenge the team to further concerted effort and celebrate with them. It is a substantial and demanding task.

What sort of person is best for a raising standards role?

If achieving massively improved results is as important as suggested, you will need the best people for the job. Putting the right people in the right jobs is easy to say but difficult to do. Traditionally this role has been thrust upon year 11 tutors. This is not a good idea. They are rarely the right people. They are not chosen for the motivational task because of skills they possess. More often than not it is for logistical reasons. Some are excellent at working on raising standards through close support but some hate it and some are not interested. Some are ill-equipped to do it. Year 11 tutors will be a mixed ability group in terms of the skills needed to raise standards. Each will have 25 or more students to look after, too many to be effective at raising academic standards. Some tutors will be interested and committed to the supportive tutoring; others will see it as an imposition 'more to do in my free time!' And if things turn out to be no better than they were before, there is no accountability demanded of them because any extra work on raising standards was all done on a good-will basis. Dealing with a matter of such importance on a good-will basis is not sensible. You can tell the importance placed on raising standards by considering two things:

- who is appointed to do it?

- how much school money is spent on it?

Other schools invite *volunteers* to join a team to monitor students. Sometimes this works well, but only if the volunteers are of the right quality and are given time. In several schools we have visited, these volunteers are well-meaning and committed but simply are too stretched to make the impact they and the school want. Some volunteers are unsuitable. The leaders in a school have to retain the right to select the best people and must find a way to avoid the inappropriate volunteer.

What qualities are needed?

What qualities are ideally suited to working in a team charged with raising GCSE scores by 10 per cent? Who are the *right people?* You will be served best by people who are:

- Driven by moral purpose

These people put students first. They are intent on making a difference and that remains the reason why they are where they are. They want what is best for students, to the point where they are prepared to challenge their own assumptions. They try to see issues from a student's point of view. Richard Branson made the startling observation about Virgin Atlantic that *we are*

not in the airline industry. We are in the entertainment industry, only at 30,000 feet. That is thinking outside the box. Teachers and other professionals who want success at GCSE for students so much that they are prepared to think beyond historic practice are well-suited to this work. This work is not doing what others are doing but discovering something different.

- Respected

Much of what follows in this book requires that students have a high regard for those people working closely with them. Sadly this is not always the case. Young people can quickly discern who cares and who does not. Being supported or encouraged by someone you believe is not really interested will have no beneficial effect at all.

- Good relationships

A significant part of the transformation depends on the ability of adults to motivate young people. Often borderline students are disengaged and disaffected and have poor motivation. To shift that position will need the ability to relate well to the student. Jack Welch (2001) said:

> If there is one characteristic all winners share, it's that they care more than anyone else. No detail is too small to sweat or too large to dream. It's something that comes from deep inside.

- Good motivators

Several teachers leading schemes in work on this agenda in London were Physical Education specialists. Sports team coaches have to have the ability to motivate. The style of motivation is not as important as the ability to motivate. The best teachers diagnose the personality of their student team members and use appropriate motivational techniques.

- Creative

Through recognising that his industry was not simply an airline industry Branson challenged his leaders to devise original and creative experiences that took account of the fact that business was advanced as much by quality entertainment as by good airline procedures. On the strength of that demand his teams introduced transformation in the airport lounge to include ski slopes, hair salons and toy train sets for young customers, along with in-flight massage and beds. The effect on business was huge when the entrepreneurs began to think creatively.

GCSEs are not just about education. For borderline students it could be argued they are much more about motivation and that means being creative about how that might be achieved.

■ Risk takers

Schools are conservative institutions. Much that happens is not radically different from years ago. The different approaches used for different kinds of students are not obvious. Teachers are often afraid to change much in case in has disastrous effects. A culture of risk-taking is relatively rare.

■ Competitive

In the chapter on Understanding Difference we explore the different ways students learn. Certainly there is a considerable body of evidence to show that competitiveness, when properly harnessed, can improve motivation in students. Similarly it can be used productively amongst team leaders. If scores for each team are recorded each week and presented in a league, there will be a winner. The best team leaders want to be winners. This can draw the best out of both the teachers and the students. It can be controlled. It need not get out of hand.

■ Systematic

Team leaders need to be well organised, systematic people. The recommendation in this book is to have teams competing against each other on the basis of scores accumulated across subjects each week. It is no good at all if the leader forgets meetings, loses papers or aggregates scores badly. The paperwork supporting the scheme needs to be thorough and reliable.

■ Doggedly determined

But there is more to it than simple operational procedures. Leaders need to be doggedly determined to cajole and challenge student team members, to chase those students who forget to meet, and encourage those who lag behind. They realise that personal contact is more important than organisational process. The best team leaders exude a positive approach in a culture of remorseless pursuit of the objective.

■ Generous with time

People take up time – hours of it. Borderline students need time to be reassured, challenged, encouraged and supported. They need time to be told they are capable, that it will be worth it and that you believe in them. The best leaders go the extra mile, take the extra hour and find the right social occasion to make their team feel special. They are not grudging, not rushing off to the next meeting. This can only be done if some allowance is made. Adding this work to an existing load is preparing the straw to break the camel's back.

■ Resilient

A new idea is delicate. It can be killed by a sneer or a yawn; it can be stabbed to death by a joke, or worried to death by a frown on the right person's brow. David Hargreaves (2003) wrote:

Innovation is a delicate plant, which thrives in a favourable climate. It grows in stages. It begins with the perception that something needs to change, stimulating the bright ideas about what might be done.

Ideas in this book will be quite new to many people. Not everybody will be in favour of spending time with borderline students. Some object on principle, believing that every student should be treated the same. Equality of opportunity is not the same as uniformity of opportunity. However, sometimes senior members of staff raise objections to new ideas, leaving the younger members in a difficult position. Resilience is vital.

■ Ready to advance their career

The gambling industry has used this concept to good effect. 'It's more interesting when there is money on it' is the way they encourage gambling linked to watching televised sport. It probably is. When something is depending on the outcome people tend to take greater interest. Business has used this principle for years through incentive payments and bonus schemes. These have been shunned in education until recently when it has become fashionable to reward headteachers for results achieved. Not many schools go as far as paying teachers for successfully discharging a specific delegated responsibility for raising standards at GCSE. However things are changing: a teacher moving up the pay spine now has to demonstrate that they have added value to students in their classes.

You may think it is appropriate to pay team leaders for the success achieved by their students, but even if you do not, team leaders are well aware of the peripheral benefits of being involved with a project that successfully delivers a substantial increase on GCSE scores. Teaching and Learning Responsibility payments, introduced in January 2006, offer an excellent opportunity to link specific financial packages to work of this kind. Teachers know that if they get this right it will do them a great deal of good – what's wrong with that as motivation to succeed?

What the school will give them

You may want to use these qualities to form a person specification for the role of team leader but you will need also to make clear what the school is going to give them so that they can do the job.

1. Direction

Socrates' equation pointed out than an essential part of empowerment in any post is a clear sense of what is expected of the post-holder. The team needs to know its job is to add 10 per cent or so to the school's GCSE performance by focusing specifically on borderline students. The big aha must not be

open to confusion, doubt or possible misinterpretation.

2. Responsibility

Autonomy was a second criterion proposed by the Socrates equation. You have the direction, now you know you have the responsibility delegated to you. No one will interfere. Henry Stewart of Happy Computers put it like this:

> I soon learnt that you can only create a second class copy of yourself if you manage yourself as a model. What you aim for is for people to feel they own their own job which means
>
> You set the principles
>
> You agree the targets
>
> You step back and let the people perform, any way they like, as long as it's within the principles and hits the targets
>
> You offer support

3. Support

Socrates spoke of the third dimension in empowerment: support. Your team knows what you want because you have given them direction. They know they have responsibility and that you will not micro-meddle in what they are doing. What they need from you is support.

Support can take the form of encouragement 'cheering louder and longer than may feel comfortable', meeting them on a regular basis to hear their news and to celebrate their success. What it does not mean is the team having to ask for approval before the work can continue, except in unusual or extreme circumstances. It can mean new resources to advance progress when it is linked to specific initiatives with a clear outcome. It can mean more time or added personnel to impact further. In short, more money needs to be focused on fulfilling the vision.

In his thesis on empowerment Socrates observed that these three characteristics are so linked that if any one is missing the effect is to make empowerment zero. That is how important support is.

4. Training

Your new team will have enthusiasm, ideas and commitment. They will not have experience or a team ethos. These need to be built. Planned training is an excellent way to do this. An after-school twilight session is as good a way as any. Recently such a session was conducted for 3 hours in London with a team of eight teachers from a school eager to begin to think about how to go about their massive challenge. They considered the issues discussed in this book in company with two other schools with experience of this work and shared ideas on how to launch their project from September 2005. Their headteacher came with them to support them but they did the planning. Having schools with positive experience to share practical ideas is helpful.

Training in this way costs money. The hire of a good quality venue, the price of a meal at the end of the session, during which informal discussion contributes almost as much as the main meeting, and sometimes costs of input from experienced people can add up to £500 or more. How inexpensive when you compare this with supply cover costs for day-time release of staff and the inefficiency of a train-and-cascade feedback model. Money spent on training is money well spent.

5. Accountability

You are supportive. They are accountable. People who have been given responsibility are usually happy to accept accountability. There has to be regular interim accountability so that the team meets formally with the school leadership on a prearranged basis to report not only on what they are doing but how it is progressing. This needs to be linked to tangible evidence, not merely impressions. Schools are good at describing what they do, not so good at evaluating what is working and what is not. It is considerably easier if measures are built into the action plan which are unequivocal and staged over the duration of the challenge, so that at the accountability sessions everyone knows whether interim targets have been hit or not. Mostly these

accountability sessions ought to be about celebration and praise but occasionally things are not progressing well enough for celebration to be appropriate. Ram Charan and Larry Bossidy (2002) wrote:

> *When we ask leaders to describe strengths and weaknesses, they generally state the strengths fairly well, but they're not so good on the weaknesses. And when we ask what they are going to do about the weaknesses, the answer is rarely clear or cohesive.*

It is important to ask what the team is going to do about missed targets and to expect a coherent answer. When you are a class teacher you are supposed to have most of the right answers: when you are a leader you are expected to know the right questions and to ask them. The spirit in which the questions are asked is important and must be supportive as well as sharp edged.

Katzenbach and Smith (1986) defined a team as:

> A small number of people with complementary skills who are committed to a common purpose, performance goals, and a common approach for which they hold themselves *mutually accountable.*

Before any accountability to senior leadership, teams will meet together to share reports and discuss progress. There should be some *mutual* accountability at this stage, for the strength of the programme is as strong as the weakest link in the team. Candour is clearly crucial.

If the team understands that it will be reporting back to governors at the completion of its assignment this could add clear focus to the planning. There is a lot of *kudos* in being responsible for outstanding success, especially when you are present when it is reported.

Training for governors on what sort of questions to ask is important. It is best if they challenge positively so that they don't inadvertently become a barrier to progress. Governors approach examination performance with a variety of attitudes:

personal involvement as a parent of a student in year 11

belief that the school can do no wrong so results will be as good as could be expected

negative perceptions of the personalities of some teachers

belief that praising teachers will make them complacent

or that criticising teachers will sharpen their performance

the view that results are a matter for the school and not the governors

sense of inadequacy about querying the performance of the school

fear that a comment may appear critical and attract disfavour from the headteacher

Good training by appropriate senior staff can address these issues. This training needs to recognise that:

- governors' opinions are important and valued highly by the school

- the inspection process requires governors to understand the examination statistics and to have an educated view about what they mean

- comparisons between the results of departments need to be made with informed judgement

- comments about individual students and teachers are to be avoided wherever possible. These matters should be addressed by the chairman and headteacher separately

- skills need to be developed so that the performance of the school, and its departments, relative to other schools in similar circumstances can be made intelligently

- data held by the Local Authority and by the school should be given to governors with appropriate analysis and explanation

- governors have a role to understand performance not to take

responsibility to bring about change in performance. This distinction between intelligent oversight of the school and day-to-day responsibility must be made clearly

- questions need to be asked. What sort of questions and how they are asked needs to be explored in depth

- follow-up is to be encouraged. When governors ask questions they have every right to expect satisfactory answers and to ensure that subsequent actions are reported back

Department heads do not mind answering questions so long as these are sensible, informed and constructive. Indeed doing so can be empowering. However, handled badly, times like this can be damaging and demoralising. It is important to get it right and you have a key part to play.

Robert Schuller asked the question, '*What would you do if you knew you could not fail?*' Probably a great deal more than you do now. But the thought of failure can create adrenaline too, especially the thought of accounting for failure. You want the team to succeed and they want to succeed. These seem like good reasons to expect success.

Action points

- Decide who will lead your raising standards initiative

- Define the qualities you want in team leaders

- Make the direction you give clear and unequivocal

- Explain the practical support team leaders will receive

- Prepare a training session before the initiative commences

- Establish the process of accountability

- Plan training for governors

- Ensure team leaders identify their own needs, seek support and receive it

Chapter 5

Through student identification

Our life is frittered away by detail... Simplify, Simplify.
Henry David Thoreau

Student identification is fundamentally important to the process of raising standards of borderline candidates. It is possible to imagine devising a brilliant series of ideas that will inspire and motivate a cohort of young people, to allocate resources and recruit the right people to almost guarantee success, yet to fail because all the effort has gone into the wrong students. Many schools have a curious relationship with data. Information about student and school performance has multiplied hugely in recent years. Most schools have seen this and established structures for managing statistics but it is not always clear how this data is used to improve the quality of learning for young people.

Over the last few years there have been considerable advances in the use of data. In fact it is a struggle not to go glassy-eyed every time the person responsible for marshalling all the school's statistics describes the organisation as being *data rich*. There is so much there that it is difficult to get at what is needed. Hawkins (2005) observed:

Many organisations embarked with great hope on the quest for Knowledge Management, only to end up with enormous data warehouses, full of well-filed data that was never accessed. A world that was pre-figured by T.S Eliot in The Rock when he wrote:

Where is the wisdom we have lost in knowledge?
Where is the knowledge we have lost in information?

It is important that we understand the difference between the various elements of knowledge hierarchy.

- Wisdom
- Understanding
- Knowledge
- Information
- Data

Learning is the process of transforming the lower elements of this hierarchy to create the higher elements. As an early Sufi poet wrote: 'Knowledge without wisdom is like an unlit candle.'

In the classroom the poor practitioner is trying to demonstrate how to use data to develop personalised learning programmes, often with more sheets with columns of figures than they could ever make sense of, or one spreadsheet covered in information in a font so small few could read it. The headings can be printed at the most acute of tangents to the figures. The guilty secret is often that everyone is convinced that all this data should be making a difference to the students. It is about data not wisdom. The accusation levelled at teachers by the data manager in school is that teachers ignore the data sent to them after it has been so meticulously compiled and stored. The teacher wonders how anyone could be so foolish as to think that the deluge of numbers they have been required to crunch would mean anything to a normally functioning human. At best, staff are selecting the things they want to focus on; at worst, a lot of hard work is being stored in cupboards and hard drives, only to see the light of day when a report needs writing or parents' evening looms. This situation is widespread, understandable, very human – and avoidable. Somehow the process of transforming the lower elements into the higher ones has to begin.

School leaders are responsible for making the link between the data office and the teachers work for the benefit of students. School leaders make the data flow in such a way that in theory staff can get anything they want, but often it is neither accessible nor helpful.

School leaders often complain at the volume of papers, figures, instructions, initiatives and funding streams that the Government channels their way. Teachers in their teams feel the same way about the data being thrown at them. The situation is capable of resolution with clear and thoughtful management. Somebody needs to yell 'stop' and then assemble the best people to think through the issue of how to use data in the school. The questions are obvious.

> What functions do you want data for?
> What specific data helps you with these functions?
> Who needs the data?
> What do you do with the data you do not need?
> How can you use the data most wisely to impact on student performance?

Most people need information to see where the organisation is most effective and where our energies need to be focused next.

Data can be used to provide information on:

- how performance compares to other similar schools

- which departments in school should have their practice celebrated and spread

- which departments need help to close a gap

- which young people are struggling and in what areas

- whether intervention programmes have been successful or not

Data can be used to highlight trends so you can plot performance and decide on what needs doing when.

You can use data to inform you about which of your teachers is strong in particular areas and which need help. You need an accurate picture of how well your teams are performing by comparison with other departments within school, and nationally. Teachers can use data to inform them about strengths and weaknesses of students and to form an impression, based on evidence, about how well they are doing against objective measures and what the next areas for their own development might be. They also need to know the profile for the young people they teach and what it tells them about the learning needs of each student.

You may identify other needs more important than these, which will ask for different forms of data. It does not matter what you choose as long as you are clear what you need and why. Then you need to choose the data that is fit for each purpose and ensure that the people who need it get it and nothing else.

The school needs to provide a data system for teachers as a fair diagnostic tool that works. Letting the data manager decide what will be useful for a teacher can mean her sending everything she already has and that, on a good day, might be useful. For some of your staff who are less logical and numerical this will be a nightmare. They will not make head or tail of the information but feel as if they should. You need to decide with the staff what will work. It may be test scores from National Curriculum end of Key Stage examinations , National Foundation for Education Research scores, Fisher Family Trust data or any other body of knowledge that is needed. In time a wider range of data may be desirable, but at the outset you need to agree what is manageable and intelligible. You need to offer training to every teacher so they can see why this data was chosen and how it may be useful to the young people they teach. You need to develop a shared understanding with them of how it fits into their daily jobs.

If you are a school leader you need to be ruthless about what is and is not admissible in terms of the way data is presented to you. A headteacher would need to be a genius at statistics to understand the wide range of models that heads of department present at meetings to review examination results. These departmental leaders come to the review meeting with data given to them by the school, which they dismiss as all but meaningless in five minutes and then produce information and analysis in a format and style of their own. The data presented puts each department in its best light. It is rare for a department's own use of statistics to make it look less successful than the official school version. This process can conceal poor practice.

This cannot be allowed to happen because several stories are being told within the school about how well departments have performed, many of which are patently untrue. It is necessary to form an agreement on the comparative data that is to be used and to refuse to countenance the introduction of any other. This may seem uncompromising, but it is fair for the same information to be used by all and for the process to be transparent. For example, if it is agreed that subject residuals are the core measurement in school for examination review purposes, people will know in advance what they need to do to make their presentation acceptable. This is important because proper analysis of the performance of students last year is important in identifying the borderline students for this year. For the school to make a transforming change it needs accurate analysis of last year's results to inform activity this year.

You need to apply rigour to the identification of students who need special help to get the results you want for them. At the outset this will need careful research. Consider carefully which set of data most accurately predicted the GCSE results last year, globally and student by student. This will vary from school to school. In my school the most accurate predictions came from teacher assessment and forecasts at the end of Year Ten. Gradually we began to wake up to the merits of raw scores in end of Key Stage examinations and NFER scores became significant, particularly with regard to potential under-achievement. Some schools identify students who might achieve 5 A* to C grades by using data provided by the Fisher Family Trust, others use level 5 in English at the end of Key Stage 3 as a good indicator of potential. Some reckon that 90+ in a verbal reasoning assessment reflects the language level needed to access intermediate papers at GCSE. If one of these measures could clearly be seen to be the perfect indicator, life would be much easier. But none of them can. We cannot work with all of them at once so it is best to decide which is likely to be of most help and go with it. There is plenty of data out there. What is needed is correct information extracted from the data leading to a knowledge of which students might achieve a grade C in which subject. Then you need wisdom about what to do!

The use of data is important as it introduces a measure of objective analysis into a process that is rightly driven by our passions and opinions. That said it is important that hard information is not the only determinant of who should be put into specific groups, borderline or otherwise. It is very useful to sit with an experienced pastoral manager who has knowledge of the students under analysis and listen to what they have to say. Very often they will look down the list of students who have not been identified as having a particular need as a borderline student and find one or two whom they know in their heart of hearts is capable of securing the grade, and they may know why the data does not reflect this. Inside information has frequently proved every bit as valuable as data.

Tracking the Students

Data can be used as a means to measure and compare performance but it is most effective when identifying trends. For this reason it is important to choose a couple of reference points in the course of the year to track the progress being made by individuals and groups, as well as the full cohort. The impact is twofold. It is possible to use it to see who is falling short of the rate of progress needed to achieve what is desirable, which can lead to varying levels of intervention throughout the year. Sometimes a young person does not respond to the service being offered as you would like. Unless there is a variable that can be isolated and removed, some other form of support must be offered. There may also be students heading for a comfortable margin of success who fall below the level that would trigger off monitoring and may need to be added to the group to get them back on track. As well as identifying those who need a different level of support at an interim stage, the data may also offer reassurance that you are heading in the right direction.

You should share the interim data as widely as possible:

- let the students see how well they are doing

- allow their parents to see what progress is being made

- share developments in detail with the staff

It is helpful to hold examination review meetings after the trial examinations to see if departments are making the progress they would like. If the results are not as good as expected it can be challenging for them, but the reality should be faced now so that bad news can be avoided when it really matters. Better to know the truth at an interim position, when help and support can be offered, than when the results come out and all that can be done is to think of excuses.

Assembling the data

Many schools assemble data on a spread sheet for the whole year group. ICT systems calculate the numbers of GCSE grade C that each student might achieve and assemble these in rank order for the group. Identifying borderline students needs care and precision.

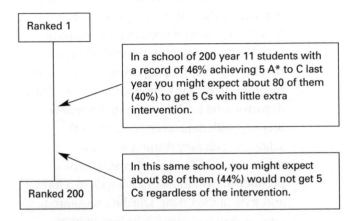

Ranked 1

In a school of 200 year 11 students with a record of 46% achieving 5 A* to C last year you might expect about 80 of them (40%) to get 5 Cs with little extra intervention.

In this same school, you might expect about 88 of them (44%) would not get 5 Cs regardless of the intervention.

Ranked 200

This means that there are 32 students 'in the middle': These are the students who will determine whether the school achieves its target or not. They amount to 16 per cent of the population. A detailed study needs to be undertaken on these students.

Detailed study

It is wise to consider *all* students individually. For the purposes of significant GCSE achievement for them, and for the school, we are considering those students who might reach 5 Cs. Details similar to the one shown below may be helpful. Using whatever data the school has, names with subjects of all 32 students should be assembled as follows:

Richard Olivier Ma (EDC), Eng (DDC), Hist (EED), Geog (DDC), Sc (EDD), PE (DDC), Art (DDC), DT (EED)

Grades shown might be: first, result in year 10 exams, second, teacher prediction based on current performance, third, teacher evaluation of potential in light of experience and external data.

It is important to calculate how many of these results represent realistic possibilities. In Richard's case it seems that he may have a good chance in 6 subjects, Maths, English (usually two subjects), Geography, Physical

Education and Art. Something could be done with Richard to enable him to achieve what will be wonderful for him. Anything less than 5 subjects predicted for achieving at grade C clearly reduces the chance of success.

In contrast, details are shown for Alicia Massoud

> Alicia Massoud Ma(EED), Eng (EDD), Hist (EED), Geog (DDC), Sc (EDD), PE (DDC), Art (DDC), DT (EED)

It is clear that for Alicia achieving 5 will be difficult. She seems to have a good chance in Geography, PE and Art, totalling 3, but the others seem long shots. She is in the middle 16 per cent but has only a small chance.

Each student should be analysed like this by a small group of teachers and with the advice of the head of year 11 or someone who knows the students well. Short of intervention from pastoral teachers who have inside knowledge, Richard would be 'identified' for help using this scheme though Alicia would not.

It is recommended that the final group chosen should be not more than 25 students in a cohort of 200. A school in this situation might aim to convert 80 per cent of those selected, which would equate to 20 students, giving an additional 10 per cent overall.

It is important to remember that these are not the most important students in the school but in terms of this particular criterion they are!

Action points

- Identify the forms of data you need and what purpose each element is for

- Collate the data identified and only distribute it to the people who need it

- Ensure that data flows in the right directions, and at the right rate throughout the year

- Train staff to use the data effectively

- Review the data with pastoral team leaders

- Focus on the borderline zone

- Determine which students will be the focus for this initiative

- Calculate the percentage impact that success would have

- Publish the target and encourage staff support

- Choose specific interim data collection points

- Share the interim results and hold review meetings

Chapter 6

Through understanding difference

To me education is a leading out of what is already there in the pupil's soul. To Miss Mackay it is a putting in of something that is not, and that is not what I call education. I call it intrusion...
Muriel Spark

An oft-quoted reflection on the ethos of British society is that we have a genius for turning diversity into hierarchy. Our traditions lead us to assume that any group which is set apart by a particular characteristic has to be judged as being of greater or lesser value. We accord all sorts of privileges and rewards to people who enjoy status that is not always of their own making, and identify any special treatment of another group as patronage, and by extension an indication that this group is more precious than ourselves. Our sense of ourselves is determined by our status and treatment in comparison to the status and treatment of others we see as different from us. It is evident in the hierarchy within schools, the groups teenagers form, hierarchies between types of school, and of sets within them.

Most educators see this tendency as intuitively wrong and give considerable thought to teaching young people to value difference without placing it on a scale. To date we have found it very difficult. Equality is extremely important to most liberal, fair-minded people and most teachers value it

highly. Thirty years ago education embraced the challenge posed by gender inequality because it was realised that girls were not getting a fair deal. They were entering school with low expectations, leaving early with very much poorer qualifications than their male counterparts and often put through a curriculum with a different content and far less status.

What a credit it is to the teaching profession that it overhauled the curriculum and assessment methods, raised the expectations of girls, demanded that fair and equal provision was given to females in school and altered its approaches to teaching so that what was valued in the way girls learn was recognised and nurtured. The result of these endeavours is that girls now outperform boys in almost every sphere of education and society has changed significantly as a result. This success is rarely acknowledged unless it is couched in terms of boys' under-achievement, but those who have contributed to this trend have good cause to be proud of what they have done. The change was difficult to make because many teachers felt that society was fine as it was and that girls were congenitally incapable of the same level of achievement as boys because of their child-bearing role and attendant emotional make-up. Those who said this were often genuine, honest, caring and intelligent people who could back their arguments up with a wealth of studies and experiences. They have since been proven wrong.

This shift, although a wonderful testimony to the power of education to change things, brought about a cultural barrier to further development in provision. The process was underpinned by a rigorous adherence to equality, which was interpreted to mean identical provision. At its best this gave all students the opportunity to follow the curriculum that best suited them, irrespective of gender. At worst it had teachers agonising over the fact that three times more girls than boys wanted to do Domestic Science and that the only girls doing Woodwork had been press-ganged by the Senior Mistress, who believed that it was only fear of intimidation by boys that had prevented the whole female cohort from wanting to be carpenters. The ethical construct that made the difference was that everyone was entitled to exactly the same treatment and the same outcomes would necessarily follow because we are all essentially identical. The equal rights of a human being are easier to sustain if it is maintained that we are the same in all key respects. Clearly this worked in the face of opposition from caring, intelligent and committed professionals who felt that the psychological, emotional and physical make-up of females meant that they were not designed for academic life and the roles in society accorded to those with higher qualifications. However it is not working for groups of our young people now.

There are a number of possible groups that may be falling short in your school. However impressive your results across the board, there will be young people with a set of characteristics in common for whom you feel you could do a better job. Nationally it would appear to be boys. Recently Trevor Phillips (2005) raised the issue of the under-achievement of black boys in schools. Those of us who care about social justice have been thinking about the issue for some time but thinking and worrying about it has been enough to ease consciences in most cases. The reason Phillips came in for such heavy criticism is because he was brave enough to

propose a solution and this meant different treatment, based on the perception of this group as having different needs and possibly different characteristics. The same can be true when you propose dealing with boys differently from girls or gifted students differently from their peers. This is for very good reasons.

The ethical framework that was used to underpin the improvements in opportunities and outcomes for girls was equality. This was based on the belief that everyone is very much the same and given the same experiences will secure the same outcome. Anyone who does not has fallen short because of some failing on their part. This implies that any attempt to put things right for boys will shift the imaginary pendulum that represents relations between males and females back in the opposite direction and women can expect to lose some of the benefits that greater social justice has conferred upon them. As a consequence, focusing on boys can be seen as a threat to the basic ideas of right and wrong in education for many people. Just as those who wanted to maintain the *status quo* were wrong to argue against change to liberate women through education, current thinking that defends equality through identity of provision need to be challenged. Trevor Phillips (2005) is right to throw the statistics in our face and force us to consider seriously what must be done to make all young people engage with education. School leaders are right to want to do something to help those they can see falling short year on year. It would be wrong of us not to consider how this can be put right. Ignoring this slippage opens the door to some unpleasant, even dangerous, ideas based on the idea of difference, be it focused on gender, race, religion, sexual orientation or any other tangible human characteristic.

The ethical basis for the work I do on improving examination performance for key groups is equal consideration of interest. This allows for the activity to be founded upon the belief that every member of the school community has an equal right to my time, effort and the resources at my disposal. However, I am not compelled to treat everyone identically as this may not be right and may even disadvantage some people. The case is made most convincingly by Peter Singer (1999), whose main thrust is the relative rights of humans and animals. It is important to outline this view as I have found teachers willing to accept it. It is founded upon care for everyone and allows people to accept pragmatic responses to unequal outcomes with a clear conscience. I am sure many of my colleagues do not accept it whole-heartedly, but they see that I have thought deeply about the issues that worry them and it stops me being seen as a hard-hearted manager who simply wants better exam results, whatever the cost to the ethos of the school.

People have different sets of needs and interests from other people. We all have an equal right to have our interests considered. If the operation of an organisation delivers what a group of people needs, its design serves their interests. Brighter students, particularly girls with good literacy and oral skills, are very well served by current provision. We can continue to operate as we do in the belief that our care for this group of young people is paying off for them. When we look at our outcomes there are groups who do far less well. It is an established trend with the reasonable prediction that if we continue to act as we do this year's boys, especially those from the black community, will be far less successful, get worse outcomes and have reduced choices as they start adult life. They will follow the path taken by older peers, which is often less happy and productive than we would like. Surely it is right that we take some time to consider their particular interests and do something to ensure that they feel as valued as those who thrive on the mainstream provision. One way of characterising the current provision is to take the default position for a student as being female. Therefore a boy can fail simply

because he does not demonstrate typically female characteristics when it comes to his learning. The problem is he is not seen as a failed girl, just a failure as a student. As for his masculinity, that is something he has to define for himself with his peers outside school, though there are ways in which his masculinity can work against his achievement given the present structure of education.

This does not make someone worthy of extra provision simply because they are male or black, or possess some other inherent characteristic. Different provision is offered because there are students who do not have their interests served as well as others in school. When you look at your results, if the trend indicates to you that girls are not doing as well as boys, you have to consider their interests in this way. The same could be true of students who appear to under-achieve whatever the difference between them and their peers.

If anything approaching a comprehensive ideal is to survive, schools will have to shift away from a one-size-fits-all approach to one that enables us to celebrate and respond to difference. Government thinking in recent years suggests that they are grasping the nettle. They are managing the perceived inability of schools to react to different needs from within their community by constructing a range of schools designed to appeal to different types of young person. Geography, culture and resources mean that it is far better to evolve ways of acknowledging reform and to recognise difference in our provision within schools than to see how a national patchwork will affect a particular region. If a school does not look to the groups who fall short, its political masters will, and the school may not be as comfortable with reforms imposed upon it as it would be with changes it made itself.

The Positive Side

This can all seem rather critical and theoretical but, once you accept the logic of the situation, it is liberating. We have groups of young people in our schools who are not thriving as they might. If you continue doing the same thing it can feel as if they are failing you as much as you them. This is the cycle you are stuck with if you find it hard to acknowledge difference. If you are able to make the shift, you can look at these groups in a completely different way. Imagine looking at the boys in your school and asking yourself the question 'What do we really value about these people that can be used to help them learn?' They stop becoming a problem and begin to present themselves as an opportunity. The schemes we have adopted for boys have been based on humour, competitiveness, group identity and the desire to hit short-term targets for immediate rewards. It is not a chore, though it is hard work and great fun much of the time. They recognise, without perhaps rationalising it, that someone is proud of them for who they are, and less time in the week is spent trying to make them conform to a structure that doesn't fit them at all. It enables teachers to think carefully about the reasons for working with young people and what we are trying to teach them beyond the exam syllabus.

The acknowledgement of the need to consider the interests of a cohort of boys who are likely to under-perform encourages teachers to think hard about the need to address difference in their teaching and vary the strategies they use to take account of it. If it is known that the leadership of the school believes that the next stage in the organisation's development is going to be greater success for boys in public examinations, staff will engage with the idea. If Continuing Professional Development (CPD) provision includes some discussion about theories concerning the ways boys and girls learn, it will underpin the emphasis being made, create conversations in the staffroom about learning in general, but boys' learning in particular, and move classroom

practice forward. It has become received wisdom now that boys do not multi-task as well as girls: they tend to be active learners, often with a kinaesthetic bent. They focus well for shorter periods of time and need instant gratification. I doubt that this is news to any teacher these days. We need to shift teaching behaviour to take account of it, at least to some extent. If boys are different from girls and we teach girls more successfully than boys, our programmes of study should develop in some ways that show an intelligent, practical and professional understanding of the learning patterns of young males and girls with male learning characteristics

In addition to developments in teaching and learning, boys are going to need some extra support beyond normal classroom routines to help them get the best from the work being done by their teachers. It would be expensive and time-consuming to offer the whole cohort monitoring, revision support, competitions and whatever other devices boys need, because then everyone has to receive everything identically. It flies in the face of common sense. However, distinct provision brings with it two problems; students who do not conform to type and the feelings of those who do not have the profile that triggers the provision.

Students who do not conform to type

Your data may demonstrate that the principal concern for the next cohort should be a particular distinct group and that there is a real chance you will be able to get a significant number of those the 5+ A* to C grades that will open up so many more choices for them. The next stage is to sit down with the key players in your teaching force and determine what characteristics this group possess that you need to work with to help them achieve their best. Occasionally someone may fall into this category who does not share these characteristics. If you consider the interests of girls in your school there may be an individual who does not feel comfortable in the company of the rest of the group. If it is boys that concern you there could be an individual who has more feminine characteristics than male. For this young man the idea of being with his peers, competing for points to go to soccer matches or go-karting might fill him with horror. It may be that he does not enjoy the company or humour of other males at all. Of course this young person has the right to have his interests considered alongside everyone else's. It is a question of common sense and balance. To decide not to offer support to the wider group for fear of upsetting one or two students who have different characteristics from the wider group is to place their interests some way below his.

One way to take account of this different need is to offer the option of taking part on an equal basis. If the student wants to be part of the scheme his wishes should be respected and a careful eye kept on his involvement by a skilled and caring individual. It may be a huge learning experience for all and enable a valuable set of relationships to develop. Should the student choose not to participate, he should receive individual support and guidance through his final year which is tailored to his needs. It is an extra drain on resources but it reinforces the notion that you are responding to the need demonstrated by the data and it emphasises your commitment to the recognition of difference. Of course this would apply equally to a girl who did not share the characteristics of others who perform similarly, students from various ethnic groups or any other student group.

The students' feelings

Should you choose to support a particular group, you will intuitively manage how they feel about being included by how you sell the scheme to them and how you set out the way the year ahead will unfold for them. Part of the narrative will inevitably involve:

- telling them how their success will feel

- outlining the enjoyable aspects of the scheme

- explaining the reasons why they are deemed important enough to be the focus of this attention

The feelings of those who are not included must not be ignored. By choosing to offer a service to one group you may be signalling not only difference but greater worth. Whenever I have employed these strategies I have found that it is vital to consider the feelings of girls in particular, for whom such patronage can often feel intensely personal. It is crucial to share the strategy with them and ask for their understanding and support. They are adept at recognising that the person speaking believes in what they are doing. They respond well to requests for support and understanding and deserve to be included in a process that is seen to be important to their school. Most respond to a mature presentation of the case with equal maturity. As ever, they will not all agree with the argument and some will still feel that they are missing something but the vast majority will accept that you care deeply about what you are doing and respect your professionalism. The fact that you make an effort to explain what you are doing as well as why and how much consideration you have given to their feelings about it will convince most of them to give you a chance.

Focusing on the group most obviously trapped at the boundary has a positive impact upon everyone's performance. A major worry when monitoring schemes are set up is that the gap between boys' and girls' performance might be closed at the expense of the advances girls have made. In our school we made ourselves and the staff a promise that if this happened we would drop the scheme because it would show that we considered the boys' interests more important than the girls'. What we sought, and got, was a win/win situation where the gap narrowed slightly, the performance of the boys improved dramatically and the girls' results went up as well. It is a pattern that repeated itself when we introduced monitoring schemes, starting with C/D boundary boys in my current school. The curriculum we deliver and the way students are examined, combined with the differences between males and females, mean that without this radical rethinking, boys will enjoy less success than their female classmates. If your results are even you should concentrate your efforts on helping girls to achieve the same value-added performance, relative to the national picture, as your boys. There are a couple of reasons for this, the first cultural, the second structural.

Cultural considerations

The boys' monitoring scheme is essentially about working on the way boys feel about themselves and their attitude to work. If a school is concerned that there is real under-achievement at the C boundary it is likely that there are a fair number of clever young people who are not as engaged with their learning as they should be. This profile of young person often has a disproportionate disruptive influence on school culture. They can see that there is not much in school for them and they are bright enough to know how to annoy teachers without going too far and confident enough not to care if they do. Any scheme that manages to make them feel more positive about their learning, and encourages them to focus on doing well has to improve the atmosphere in lessons, which in turn has a major spin-off for their classmates.

Structural considerations

Few people would take issue with provision for students with special educational needs. Quite rightly these young people deserve a different kind of care from their peers and often considerably more care. It is frequently argued that a deeper interest in supporting special needs students has benefited the wider student population, based upon the proposition that thinking about the learning needs of an individual inevitably brings about developments in practice that help many others. This view has merit and applies

equally well to consideration of any other specific group. Teachers thinking about the learning of boys and the nature of their relationships with them will operate in subtly different ways that will benefit all. Professional practice develops when teachers think about the nature and impact of their work and this development is bound to improve quality for all. The other students will also recognise that the young people we begin to work with to counter under-achievement are often those who spoil their learning opportunities. If it is seen that we care enough about these characters to want to offer them more of our time and effort then it is clear that we care about everyone.

The Able, Gifted and Talented

How to handle gifted students is an additional and perhaps more difficult dilemma for many in education. Those of us who have worked in schools given extra money under the government's *Excellence in Cities* initiative have had to debate these issues for a few years now. This is because finance was provided specifically to work with gifted and talented students. An early decision to be taken, once the school has identified the cohort, is whether or not to tell the students themselves or their families that they were perceived to be more gifted or talented than their peers. The arguments against telling students are:

- teachers are concerned that knowing they are gifted might make young people arrogant

- being identified as gifted might put extra pressure on them

- young people who have been left off the Gifted and Talented register may feel themselves to be of less value

- parents of those not included on the gifted register may raise difficult questions about the identification procedure

- what if the register changes and someone may have to be removed from the identified group at a later stage, causing considerable distress

- expectations will be raised that a school could not reasonably meet

Some colleagues find it socially and politically difficult to direct a greater proportion of their care to young people who are perceived to have it all going for them anyway, who often come from a socially advantaged background and who are going to be successful in any case. Unlike special needs students, or those under-achieving at the boundary, those who are acknowledged as being significantly more academically able than their peers are in danger of being seen as more valued and better as people because society perceives them that way. Students also know that many teachers value academic ability and have a natural inclination to respond positively to those who possess it.

It can be argued that looking after the interests of very able children as a separate group places the interests of those without such a high level of academic intelligence below those of their peers. Bright children are not necessarily better or more important than any others. Many are delightful company, but more than a few can be difficult to work with. In nature and temperament they are as varied as any other group, but they have a significant characteristic of being gifted that really should be addressed. If your data suggests that your value-added performance at the top end of your school's ability profile is as high as it is for the rest of the school then it is not wise to use this as a place to start raising standards. If you look at your results and identify your most able young people as a group that appears to perform less well than their counterparts nationally it is just as wrong to ignore this as it is to ignore the under-achievement of any other group. Gifted children confront their own set of challenges as they grow up that might even outweigh their advantages. It cannot be right to ignore their needs. If a school offers a curriculum that every student has to follow, it will serve some students badly. Results often show that

gifted students can also do less well than they might in a one-size-fits-all environment. Additionally, more able children have an opportunity to leave school and make a difference in a way, and on a scale, that their peers usually do not. A community needs its most able people to function at least as well as the brightest people elsewhere.

When discussing what made our brightest young men different from their peers we found two distinct groups. One performed well in public examinations while the other did not. The former group achieved very good examination results, often out-performing the brightest girls. Their academic strength was often in the logical areas of the curriculum Mathematics, Chemistry, Physics and Computing and they tended to eschew more creative and socially demanding areas like Art or Drama. These young people were loners, who had decided early on not to be part of the mainstream. Often they formed a very small group with young men of a similar disposition that was considered at best 'odd' by their peers. The support which benefited them was often specific academic help that enabled them to work through a particular problem in a specific topic. Supporting them as individuals in a one-to-one situation with a teacher they liked gave them a great deal of personal reassurance. They were included in the wider scheme because it was healthy for them to work more closely with other boys and for their team mates to gain some understanding of them.

The second group were slightly less able than the first but more likely to be polymaths. They were sociable, more inclined to enjoy typically male pursuits like sport, and were more extrovert. Unlike the first group they were concerned abut peer pressure and had made great efforts not to be viewed by the other boys as 'swots'. This peer pressure can be used to improve the attainment of boys like this.

Once it was clear that a significant difference could be made with brighter boys, our next challenge was the bright girls in our care. Typically they were sociable. They mixed well with most other girls and bright boys, and formed a close network of able girls without assistance from adults. They communicated with each other a great deal and managed their relationships with teachers well. They valued academic achievement. They were collaborative, supporting each other impressively. They worried about work and workload, they often overworked and almost always felt they were doing too much and spent hours longer on a task than boys who secured the same level of marks.

Our scheme involved each young woman working with a member of staff on a one-to-one basis. The focus of mentoring sessions was problem-solving rather than discussions about how well things were going. A group of girls working together often became an unburdening session discussing stress related to workload, teachers who did not like them and unreasonable parents. They presented themselves as uniquely miserable and sinking fast. At the end of the session they announced how much they enjoyed the process and bounced off together with a cheery wave, leaving the mentor inconsolable and any issues unresolved. That was our experience! However, one-to-one meetings enable the mentor to:

■ find out what the particular problem is

■ focus on ways to solve the issue

■ make representations to teachers on behalf of the students

■ help with time management

■ provide solutions that remove the cause of stress

We found boys worked well to SMART targets (that is targets Specific, Measurable, Achievable, Realistic and Time constrained) but that this was not so effective for girls. For them we asked teachers to produce what we called subject focuses. These were specific skills present in A* work that was not demonstrated by students achieving grade B. This meant that the teacher must have a clear understanding of the difference and be able to communicate to the young person. The student could then produce a piece of work targeted at the highest level, which often meant a higher mark for less work than they were used to doing.

None of the approaches are at all complex: they are based upon common sense. Clever people thought hard about difference and how best to address it in an educational context. The same strategy can be applied to different ethnic groups, those with significantly different social and economic profiles or any other group in your school whose results identify them as having a common identity academically and who share other characteristics. The hardest part is taking the intellectual step of acknowledging that different profiles require different provision and being determined to provide it.

Society has become more sophisticated and diverse and education is in a strong position to deal with this. In acknowledging and celebrating difference, while liberating it from any sense of hierarchy, you need to concentrate on the interests of those who appear to be in greatest need. It is to be hoped that we are now secure enough in our conviction that we can make a difference for particular groups without sacrificing the premise that all people are of equal worth. Those who are destined to do less well than others are worthy of special consideration. You will not be able to help them unless you acknowledge what makes them different.

Action points

- Explain to all students the difference between equality of opportunity and uniformity of opportunity emphasising the professionalism of teachers in addressing difference

- Identify the groups of students who are doing least well in examinations against similar candidates elsewhere

- Determine with key people in school what are the shared characteristics that distinguish this group

- Devise a scheme that uses and celebrates these differences

- Ensure that those affected understand what you intend to do and, most importantly, why

- Monitor the impact of the scheme on all students

- Evaluate the outcomes and identify key learning points

"Son, your mother is a remarkable woman."

Chapter 7

Through motivation

Innovation is a change that creates a new dimension of performance
Peter Drucker

Innovation is learning to do things differently in order to do things better
David Hargreaves

When the salesman returned to his office after a poor series of results he had a meeting arranged with his boss. In order to explain his poor performance he said,' You can take a horse to water but you can't make it drink.' The manager was unimpressed. He exploded, 'Drink! Your job is not to make them drink, your job is to make them thirsty.'

You hear that same reasoning at examination result review time. It means *we* did all *we* could, it was the students who did not deliver. It misses the point that perhaps we were not able to motivate the students in a way that was productive. In any school there are some students who are well motivated. Surrounded by enthusiastic friends and encouraged by parents these people are fully engaged in school. They are a joy to teach and often they achieve well. Borderline students have friends too but often with considerably less enthusiasm for education. They enjoy the social interaction offered by school but have little interest in academic achievement. If

they are given encouragement by parents it meets with apathy. They are unmotivated.

It is not enough for professional people to imply 'it's them not us.' Certainly some students are unresponsive to the best endeavours but too little thought has been given to what might motivate students and what we the professionals can do to motivate them. Teachers spend hours talking with students like this, cajoling, advising, mentoring, challenging and disciplining them in the hope that they will become more engaged with school. We did that too – with limited success. It is frustrating work. We began to wonder whether we were trying to get the ideas of qualified academic middle class people into the heads of young people whose thinking was entirely different from that. Do we do that in life outside education?

'Eggs are good for you', I told my one year old son when I was urging him to eat his boiled egg. After the first mouthful he was not keen to have more. I used my most persuasive techniques. I told him how good eggs were for growing people. I told him the egg would make him strong and healthy. I told him little white lies: it will make your hair curl. I resorted to bribery: if you eat this we will have some ice cream. Unforgivably, the final resort is to threaten, 'You will sit there all day unless you eat this egg.' It all fell on deaf ears in my house. Maybe it was bad parenting skills. In the end we made aeroplanes from pieces of toast, dipped them in the egg and proceeded to make silly noises and fly these things up in the air. It often worked like a dream. Once we concentrated on what interested *him* he followed the path of these aeroplanes right into his own mouth! It was the outcome I wanted, for reasons that were his. Denny (2004) distinguishes between manipulation and motivation. Manipulation, he argues, is getting somebody to do something because *you* want them to, whereas motivation is getting somebody to do something because *they* want to.

Schools have good things they want the students to do. There is no doubting the benefits of what they have to offer. The problem is that the student does not see it that way. I have come to the view that for many of them, at this time in their life, they never will. You can give them all your reasons, you can resort to bribery: *if your coursework is handed in I will give you no more homework for a fortnight;* or to threats: *if your coursework is not handed in you will be in detention for the next three Thursdays to do it.* Perhaps you need to learn how to make aeroplanes.

This approach has been called WIIFM, the 'what's in it for me' argument. It sounds selfish and not of high enough moral value. Yet, argues Warren Bennis, for any vision to be achieved there has to be attractiveness in it as well as an appeal to self-interest. You need to be careful about occupying the moral high ground when according to him most of us need to have self-interest in any vision to make it successful. Could it be that what you offer and the way you promote it to borderline students, and maybe others too, fails to create sufficient attractiveness or self-interest in them? If that is so, what can be done that might have a better effect? Biggs and Moore (1993) identified four types of motivation:

- Extrinsic: the task is carried out because of negative or positive reinforcing consequences

- Social: the task is carried out due to the appeal of influencing people

- Achievement: the task is carried out for the pleasure of success and future prospects

- Intrinsic: the task is carried out because I want to do it for its own sake.

Schools are excellent with students with intrinsic motivation and use all the others to a lesser or greater degree. Borderline students may well be most influenced using extrinsic and social motivation techniques. The ideas proposed here develop strategies using these two concepts.

Theory of motivation

What do you believe will motivate borderline students? They are not all the same, of course, but there are some common features that need to be considered. The majority of borderline students are boys. About 10 per cent more girls achieve 5 good GCSE grades than boys. Some schools take pride in the fact that they buck this trend. That may indeed be praiseworthy but given the widespread view that in the present system of examining girls are more likely to outperform boys, it may be worth asking whether the girls in these schools are themselves underperforming.

This is what we discovered about boys: they are motivated by:

- short term targets

- competitive challenges

- acknowledgement of their sense of humour

- working in teams rather than on their own

- defined tasks that they believe are achievable

- peer interest, support and pressure

- tangible reward and celebration

- close personal attention to their team

- help with their organisation

- reporting back on short-term success

If you give the same coursework to a group of boys and girls, the usual response is for girls to draft and redraft, to have the work completed in advance of the deadline and to present it all in a meticulous format. Boys, on the other hand, typically leave it to the last minute, or exceed the deadline, do one version with no redrafting and present it whatever its condition. They do not bother with refinements or niceties. Of course, there are exceptions but this pattern happens across the country. It is no good giving boys a long-term goal without providing intermediate steps and interventions. We recommend you to use a motivational scheme taking this *short-term* attitude into account. The procedure we propose does that.

Most boys thrive on *competitive challenges*. At least they do when they have a chance of winning. There is no fun at all engaging in a battle that you cannot win. This is what disengages many male students: they do not believe they have a chance of winning in the school situation. This is a significant de-motivator. I learned this lesson coaching rugby where just occasionally a physically weak student would be confronted by a huge athletic player. It's not funny. If it was to happen week in and week out you might wonder how long the weaker student would keep coming to P.E. lessons. It must feel like that for some boys in school lessons. On all the competitive issues, and that is often how they see it, they cannot win. They do not get merit awards because there are so many more people better placed to get them on the basis of the criteria used, they are not highly placed on the academic ladder and rarely achieve recognition. They are often damned with faint praise, no doubt given with the intention of trying to motivate them. They appear ordinary and they feel ordinary. They are known well only if they misbehave. When they don't, their names are sometimes forgotten. These people need to be motivated by engaging in a competition they can win. They need to have the chance to be recognised for their achievement.

By contrast, girls generally prefer collaboration to competition. They like to talk things through. They do not seek solutions in the same way that boys do. Typically at break-time in schools boys rush outside to a tennis court or play area and create teams. Younger boys pretend their teams are Brazil and England and they play football as though they were. They play until the bell, and beyond. They return to class sweaty and dishevelled talking about the winning goal. It matters a great deal. It is taken very seriously. Sometimes it results in fights! Girls, on the other hand, drift out of class at break and assemble in small groups to talk. They talk all break-time and only arrive back when they have spent too long doing their hair in the school toilets. We know that not all boys and girls are like this but quite a few are. Can these traits which are clearly attractive to the people following them be used in motivating students when in class? For these reasons we advocate using teams for boys to work competitively with short-term targets and for girls to work collaboratively, talking through issues that you want them to talk about.

With boys in particular you could *create teams*. Boys like humour and respond well to appropriate uses of it. Indeed, funny boys often add considerably to the quality of lessons. The teams you create might have names, a bit like Brazil and England in football, but with a tinge of humour. Finding something that gives boys an identification of their own is helpful. A team of five boys is a manageable size. Each team should have a staff leader and a male student leader working alongside the member of staff. Boys like working in teams. They respond better to the pressure provided by their mates than by teachers. Typically, boys like to impress and please their friends and if there is a choice between pleasing them and pleasing a teacher they will go with their peers. If this is true, you need to use it. Putting boys in teams to compete with each other will give the boys chance to *impress their peers*.

Subject report pages   for Student's name......................................

Team...............

Subject: Mathematics   Teacher's name:..

Meeting Time	-3	-2	-1	0	+1	+2	+3
20 Jan	▓	▓				▓	▓
3 Feb	▓						▓
24 Feb							

Figure 1

Boys will *rise to a challenge* if it is well defined and they believe it is achievable. The teams that you create need to know that they have a realistic chance to excel. On no account should you include achievement in the competition. Achievement for borderline students is an area of perceived failure. That is not how teachers see it of course but it is how it feels for many borderline students. By contrast anyone can *make an effort*. Trying hard is within anyone's capabilities no matter what their history. From a teacher's perspective increase in effort will automatically make a difference to achievement. You will get what you want by giving the students an incentive to be involved in an activity that is possible for them. Combining measuring effort with the importance of having short-term targets leads to constructing a competitive system to record changes in effort on a weekly or fortnightly cycle, with tangible rewards for the team winners every cycle.

The scoring system we recommend is to score each student in every subject on a scale of minus one to plus one, minus one meaning the effort has been worse this week than last, zero means it is much the same and plus one means it has improved over the past week. It is a simple but clear system. It can be badly abused! Some teachers seem to enjoy scoring students at minus ten: they had a bad week!

This must not be allowed because it ruins the competitiveness of the competition. If you are so far behind you lose interest. Equally, you should not allow plus ten for those who have been brilliant. Some teachers are reluctant to comply but you should insist. In figure 2 (opposite) the shaded spaces indicate prohibited areas and may help focus teachers' attention on what is not allowed! Denny (2004) said hope is the criterion for people to be motivated. Hope of winning is a significant part of this scheme. Many of these borderline students have little hope of academic success. It vanished long ago. However, achievement will come if you can encourage effort through creating hope.

A typical student sheet on which all these scores are recorded is shown as figure 1 above. This is with a fortnightly cycle.

You would produce a booklet like this for each student for each subject. A proforma suitable for this is provided on the CD with this book and is shown on the pages in the appendices under the heading Creating Success.

The student is required to get this sheet completed by the subject teacher each cycle. It may look like the one shown in figure 2. The asterisk represents the teacher's initials. The system demands minimal administration from teachers and yet makes significant impact. The shading indicates areas where a signature may not be placed.

Subject report pages   for Student's name...

Team...............

Subject: Mathematics   Teacher's name:..

Meeting Time	-3	-2	-1	0	+1	+2	+3
20 Jan	▓	▓			*	▓	▓
3 Feb	▓			*			▓
24 Feb					*		

figure 2

Figure 2 shows that the student improved his effort in maths in the fortnight leading up to 20 January, regressed in the next period of time and then improved consistently over the next weeks. These scores are obviously going to be the focus for discussion between the teacher leading the team and the team members themselves. When these scores are then put together in a phase score sheet as shown in figure 3, they are a clear focus for comparison between the efforts made by some in contrast to that made by others. Working on the basis that effort is a quality that all can demonstrate, it usefully makes significant points to students.

The phase score sheet is constructed by interpreting the scores shown on sheets as in figure 2. The numerical score is the

Phase score sheet

Subject	First score	Second score	Third score	Phase 1 total
Mathematics	1			
English (*2)	0			
Biology	1			
Chemistry	-1			
Physics	0			
Option A	1			
Option B	-1			
Option C	1			
Option D	1			
Religious Studies	0			
Physical Education	1			
Other subject	0			
Organisation	3			
Total	7			

figure 3

Team score sheet

Team:...............................

Subject	Student 1	Student 2	Student 3	Student 4	Student 5	Total
Mathematics	1	1	0	1	1	4
English (*2)	0	2	-2	0	2	2
Biology	1	1	0	-1	1	2
Chemistry	-1	-1	0	1	0	-1
Physics	0	0	-1	1	0	0
Option A	1	1	1	1	1	5
Option B	-1	1	1	0	1	2
Option C	1	1	0		1	3
Option D	1	0	0			1
RS	0	1	-1	-1	-1	-2
PE	1	1	1	1	1	5
Organisation	3	3	3	1	3	13
Total	7	11	2	4	10	34

figure 4

movement since last time, namely plus one means greater effort. In this example the student has made more effort in Mathematics, Biology, Option A, Option C and Option D and in P.E. but has regressed in Chemistry and Option B with no change in the other subjects. In addition, you will notice that Organisation is rewarded. You will find that some borderline students are badly organised. Instead of using sanctions, it is proposed that an incentive approach is more likely to succeed. If students get a score in every space on their sheet they qualify for three points. If they do not, they get a proportionately lower score from a teacher, depending on how many are missing. The scheme needs to be based around positive incentive rather than confrontation and discipline. For that reason it is best to avoid contracts and reports. The booklet of these sheets needs to be designed so there is no resemblance to disciplinary reports currently used in the school.

Peer pressure is a substantial motivator, particularly for boys, and so the boys in a team meet the team leader and the student team leader to share their scores with each other and have them recorded on an overall sheet, as shown in figure 4.

It is important to have a meeting room that is:

quiet and uninterrupted

comfortable

suitable for a group meeting of seven people

The meeting begins with each team member sharing their own scores in front of everyone else, during which time the team leader writes them on the overall score sheet as shown in figure 4. Clearly there is peer pressure in this situation. Because all team members know that this is a team competition, the scores of one boy impacts on the scores of all the others. In an evaluation conducted at Douay Martyrs School, Hillingdon, one boy wrote, 'I got good scores because I didn't want to be the one who let the team down.' Higher

League Table

Team	Score 1	Place 1	Score 2	Place 2	Score 3	Place 3	Total Score	Final Place
Team 1	34	3						
Team 2	38	1						
Team 3	29	5						
Team 4	31	4						
Team 5	37	2						

figure 5

motivations exist but this one was strong enough to produce good results for a borderline student.

It is important to remind the team that this is a competition about effort and that everyone can improve on effort. You are not asking the impossible. In this illustration it is clear that students 3 and 4 are letting the team down. It is here that help can be offered. The discussion which follows means that all the boys can discuss what is going wrong and both the team leader and the student team leader can see in which subjects there is a problem. The team can decide there and then what help can be offered to make sure this does not happen again. Of course, sometimes it does happen again. Not all young people respond to this approach but experience has shown that well over 90 per cent of them do. A wise team leader will investigate with the subject teacher what the problem is for any one student in their subject. This intervention is meant to help the student to address the difficulty. Typical responses are 'he's not doing his homework' or 'he distracts others'. Once this is ascertained, it can be reported to the student by the team leader who made the enquiry. Unfortunately not all teachers are good at explaining to students why they treat them so negatively, nor do they make plain to them exactly what they must do to improve. Intervention by a third party can be helpful for both teacher and student. If you feel that it is too detailed for each student to record the

individual scores of other team members, it may be enough for each student to record the total score achieved by each of their team colleagues – though the team leader will need more detail for follow up purposes.

These overall scores are then submitted to the Raising Standards Team leader who assembles them on a sheet, as in figure 5. This would happen fortnightly.

Team 1 scored 34 points, transferred from figure 4. The scores from the other teams are transferred in a similar way. The students in team 2 will celebrate and will receive a tangible reward for being first, maybe music tokens, other vouchers or cash prizes. One school offered book tokens, which was not a good idea! Rewards need to be what students value not what we wish students would value. They are meant to be an incentive. The difference between reward and celebration is that when there is a reward it motivates for *this* activity, when there is a celebration it motivates for the *next* activity. That is why after the assembling of the results, all the teams need to be brought together for a celebration where the results are announced, in reverse order to maximise the drama. This was done with significant impact by the leaders in Hendon School, who created palpable tension and excitement when scores were read out. After the announcements are made, team leaders meet their teams and review the situation. In the case of team 1 above who scored 34 coming third, analysis indicates that if students 1, 3 and 4 had scored two more points each or if 3 and 4 had just been more organised, their team would have won. No matter – what can we do about it? The student team leader says 'I will help you get organised. I will remind you the day before scores are due in and chase you round to make sure all are in.' The team leader sees students separately to report back on the personal research she did about what subject teachers expect from students and asks to see the student's homework in that subject before it gets handed in. It is support, encouragement, focused and targeted on areas of weakness to create success for students.

You will see from figure 4 that there are spaces for three rounds or phases. Scores in the first two phases should stand alone, so that a team winning phase one does not carry that advantage into phase two. At the end of the three phases the overall scores are added to create the winner of the final. This merits a significant and substantial reward. Schools have gone go-karting with the team leader taking part too. Now there is a therapeutic activity where a teacher can learn what it is like not to be the best in the class! Others have given tickets to concerts or football matches. It does not matter so long as it is what the students are keen to win.

This scheme occupies six weeks. At the end the team leaders need to meet to analyse the strengths and weaknesses of the programme. The outcome might be

Change the team members because some teams were so far behind they are unlikely to be competitive. Students soon lose interest when they know they have no chance. Remember hope is essential to motivation. The Football League knows this: some years ago they introduced the play-offs. No doubt there was strong financial incentive but from a spectator's point of view it added interest because it meant that even when you knew there was no chance of being first or second maybe you could come sixth and still get promoted through the knock-out play-off

route. It meant that for most teams the season was not meaningless for four months or more. This is about motivation and it has paid huge dividends. It retains hope.

Move some students out because they do not like the scheme. These are likely to be few but students in this scheme must be volunteers. They need to be told about the benefits and opportunities. They need to have what's in it spelled out for them. They need to have an attractive picture painted around those things that are of interest to them but then they need to be willing conscripts not pressed people.

Add students into the scheme. There may be space created by students moving out or you may decide to expand the scheme. Other students and their parents are likely to ask if their children can join. You need to be clear. It is advisable not to take students who are not in this borderline group because to do so diminishes the impression that this is something special and in any case you may introduce students of considerably more ability and implicitly introduce the achievement agenda when your emphasis has been on the effort agenda.

It is important to remember the underlying principles. This is a motivational scheme. Anything that reduces the motivational influence on these key marginal students needs to be avoided. The team leaders need constantly to return to the question 'What do we believe?' and ensure that everything they are planning has a strong theoretical basis.

Some schools have introduced other prizes as well as the team rewards in order to promote hope and involvement. Awards could be made for:

- highest individual score
- highest score in each team
- most improved students
- most improved team

The final two are particularly powerful as they can be used to stimulate the interest of those who have not progressed well so far. Anything that adds motivational influence is worth considering.

How are teams selected?

In the chapter on student identification it was made clear how to create a group which we are calling borderline or key marginal students. Let us suppose there are 30 students. Remember the aim is for at least 60 per cent of them getting 5 A* to C grades in the summer GCSE next year. These 30 students will be guided, encouraged and supported by six teacher leaders and by six student leaders. These student leaders may be drawn from the 30 students but it is wiser to select them from those students in the year group who have excellent leadership potential or from year 12. Hendon School selected twelve teachers to lead six groups so that they were able to double up. This was highly successful but is quite unusual. However, it is brilliant preparation for the future, providing a reservoir of leadership potential for another initiative.

The combination of teachers and student leaders hold a meeting with the list of 30 students in the borderline scheme on the table. They discuss what the principles are for selecting students to teams to have most impact. These are likely to be:

- Who do you know well?
- Who do you think you can influence?
- Who ought not to be in a team with which other students?
- How can you create balanced teams?

One way to proceed is to take turns in choosing from the list so that each leader and student leader end up with students they believe they can support, and with teams which appear to have a reasonable chance of succeeding.

Making the most of student leaders

This is a serious responsibility as well as a glorious opportunity to develop leadership skills. You ought to prepare a job description for students undertaking this role. It might contain some of the following actions:

- support and encourage team members
- check that they are completing their forms
- meet with the teacher leader to devise support strategies
- keep an eye on team members in lessons they share
- help my team to be well organised
- make my team aware of meetings
- challenge my team to excel
- report back to the team leader with information or advice
- check that organisational paperwork is in good order
- congratulate my team when it is doing well
- stay behind after school to support team members who need help
- make sure my team meet their coursework deadlines

Some students are well-suited to such a role and could have an extraordinary influence. But they need to be trained and developed. One way to do this is by having an after-school training session for a couple of hours, led by a skilled trainer, with all prospective student leaders and the teacher leadership team. This should be followed by a team-building visit to Pizza Hut or somewhere attractive to students. Where student leaders have been particularly successful, there is opportunity for an outstanding contribution to their Record of Achievement. All student leaders might be expected to have something impressive in their file through this sort of work. It can contribute hugely to the success of other students. It fits well with the Citizenship agenda and has the potential to develop moral purpose in young people: this is truly making a difference for others. Some schools have used students in the sixth form as student leaders and proposed that evaluation of their work would form the basis of a section on their university application form or for references for future study or employment. This was attractive to students and a powerful motivation to make their work successful.

David Hargreaves (2003) argued that:

> We must all acknowledge the limits of central interventions and capitalise on the power and commitment of the professionals and others with local knowledge to work the magic that makes a sustained and disciplined transformation. If teachers are to take ownership of reform through innovation in their practices, they must play a part in their creation.

These ideas are starters. As Jack Welch (2005) put it about General Electric: *We celebrated people who not only invented things, but found great ideas anywhere and shared them with everyone in the company. We believe that everybody should be searching for a better way. This kind of company is filled with energy, curiosity and a spirit of can-do.*

A school that engages with the vision to improve by around 10 per cent at GCSE and engages its best people to make it happen can also be filled with energy, curiosity and a spirit of can-do. It can happen and it's exciting when it does.

Action points

- Work out what you believe about boys

- Work out what you believe about girls

- Decide on a motivational scheme based on what you believe

- Brief teachers fully and carefully on the system to be implemented and its moral purpose

- Decide whether to use student leaders and who they should be

- Write a clear job profile with specific direction and indications of support to be offered

- Prepare training for student leaders using highly skilled professionals

- Work out how much money will be allocated to rewards and what these might be

IT'S ALWAYS 'GOOD DOG'— NEVER 'GREAT DOG.'

GREGORY

Chapter 8

Through coursework

Every man's work, whether it be literature or music or pictures or architecture or anything else, is always a portrait of himself
Samuel Butler

Coursework is a crucial part of success in external examinations. Finding a way to get students to hand in work that is a true reflection of their ability is difficult. The number of assignments handed in across all subjects in the course of an academic year is daunting. Management of all those deadlines, with different lengths, assessment methods and weighting can be very challenging. School leaders rarely have convincing control over this process. This is surprising because it significantly affects the lives of those teaching and studying GCSEs and has a massive impact on the outcomes by which the school as a whole is judged. It is the area where many borderline students struggle. In fact, the analysis of results by subject component often shows that many young people who might have got a grade C or higher have failed before they walk into the examination hall because they have under performed in their coursework to a degree they could never hope to compensate for in an examination.

I have sat through many meetings with Heads of Faculty as we debrief the results and look at things that were less successful than they might have been. A recurring theme was coursework; the time it took, the hassle it caused and the negative impact it had on students at the boundaries, particularly boys. It prompts analysis of what goes wrong for teachers, students and school leaders and how we might manage the situation so that it does not cause so much stress and disappointment for those we work with.

The usual problems
Most schools experience similar problems:

- coursework is not completed by the deadline

- students feel pressured by several teachers at the same time

- coursework is presented in its final form, not first in draft

- several students have presented no coursework

- lack of self-discipline means work is rushed to meet deadlines and the quality is poorer than it could have been

- teachers are stressed and relationships with students strained by the need to get coursework in

- students claim that coursework has been handed in and lost by the subject teacher

Teachers complain that they always give plenty of time to coursework and set deadlines well in advance. When asked how it is going, students do not complain that there is a problem, so it is expected in on time. When it is due in, a large proportion is missing and much of what is there is sadly disappointing. Then the process of chasing it begins. Students claim they are working flat out on pieces of work for other subjects, that several substantial assignments were expected in at the same time and they are staying behind after school every night completing work for another department. Some departments seem to have young people doing coursework solidly for much of the final year. Several students take time off school, ostensibly to complete the coursework, but absences seem designed to avoid handing it in. Extension after extension is granted, usually by a number of departments for the same students. It often feels easier to get an audience with the Queen than to get these young people to a detention, as they are booked up for weeks with other teachers. At some point teachers give up on certain of their students and the coursework mark reflects neither the quality of the student's intellect nor the commitment of the member of staff.

Demands of coursework

Students often consider the demands of coursework schedules to be unfair. They claim that they did not get enough help with it, that the deadlines all seem to arrive within a week of each other and that they are de-motivated because they go from lesson to lesson being nagged by teachers demanding overdue coursework. The point comes where some youngsters are swamped by it all and ignore the problem in the hope that it will somehow go away, or they give up completely. Those who can be relied upon to produce a high standard of work, in sufficient quantity and on time complain that they often work into the small hours to meet a deadline that other people miss with no apparent consequence whatever.

School leaders become frustrated at the annual repetition of the identical refrains. The same approach appears to have been used year upon year, with the same results, which nobody wanted. The problem was not expressed until it was too late for senior leadership to do anything about it and no remedy appears to be proposed that would prevent this year's cohort from suffering the same fate as its predecessors. In fact teachers seem to imply that the problem sits somewhere between the students and the leadership of the school, with no sense of irony at all. In truth they are half right.

If you are conscious that an undesirable cycle is about to repeat itself, surely you should be looking for radical solutions to the problem. Teachers worry about the situation and it creates a lot of work for them without a great deal of recognition. It is upsetting for many to acknowledge that they are not getting the right quantity and quality of work from students and the best of teachers take this personally. You ought to be looking for ways to support them in their attempts to get work that they and the pupils concerned are pleased with. It has to have a positive effect on the well-being of all concerned. Otherwise there is a serious and acknowledged weakness built into the routine of the school that everyone is pretending does not exist.

A headteacher wants all the young people in their school to produce coursework that is a true reflection of their ability. This is particularly true of those young people who fall most short in this area, who tend to be the borderline students. She wants an accurate picture of how well coursework is going across the year group and to reduce the stress that is caused by missed deadlines. The senior leadership team has to take responsibility for this. Departmental autonomy creates a structure that has teams working in competition against each other for the attention of the crucial students. This also means that there is a duplication of effort, with a relatively small number of students tying up a disproportionate amount teachers' time.

A central coursework submission system

One solution is to arrange for all coursework to be handed in to one place. For this to happen, the person receiving the coursework has to have an accurate picture of who owes what and when. Teachers need to submit their exact deadlines so that the class list can be ready in advance and names checked off as assignments come in. This has two indirect advantages. The first is that the senior leadership team can see the rate at which coursework is due in. This enables them to see points in the calendar that are too crowded. Although students can be guilty of crying 'wolf' over the workload at certain points in the year, there will be times when the number of assignments due in does seem unmanageable. This is something that can be discussed and managed at the level of departmental leadership once you have a complete and accurate picture.

The deadlines that teachers submit must be exact. They do not have to coincide with a lesson because the students are handing it to someone who does not teach them. In fact the teacher might like a day or two to go through the submissions before they meet the students. It is better if larger departments do not choose the same day for every teacher as this creates a huge task for the person receiving the work and students waiting to have assignments checked off may be late for lessons. Another benefit of this approach is that teachers are then bound to stick to the deadline. They are not tempted to grant extension after extension to individuals or classes. Students have to get extensions from the coursework co-ordinator, who might ask for a letter from home before granting it, so parents are made aware that there is a problem and there is less chance that students will be tempted to be economical with the truth. The teacher does not have the pressure that goes with saying no and colleagues know that the time that students should be spending on their work is not going on another subject's long overdue assignment. A full schedule of deadlines can be published early on, showing the titles of the work due and the exact date that each teacher expects it in. This is published for staff, students and parents. Some teachers argue that a central system causes a loss of autonomy, but there are widespread benefits.

What to do about defaulters

Students missing deadlines have to be dealt with immediately. They have a day to explain their failure to submit the work to the central office before the Senior Leadership Team respond. A letter should go home saying that the student concerned is staying back after school to complete the work. The student is then forced to stay back every night until the work is in. It will cause some conflict in a few cases but it is with the designated member of the Senior Leadership Team and not several teachers. You have sufficient authority to be able to insist on compliance or impose severe sanctions on the offender, teachers are not spending hours on a stressful task, relationships in the classroom are not compromised by persistent chasing of work and teachers feel supported by the direct involvement of the school management with GCSE candidates.

For the students concerned it is tough. They will feel picked on and there will be a couple of weeks of hard work on their part and yours. However, the work will come in, for some a pattern of getting it done will establish itself and you will know who is struggling, where they are finding it difficult and how many young people will need this kind of attention throughout the year. The students concerned will avoid the much worse problem of owing a large number of pieces, with the final deadline looming and no hope at all of putting together a profile of work that truly reflects what they are capable of. Parents will be informed of the problems their child is having, and will have time to respond supportively. In addition the young people who manage their time and commit themselves to their work can see the consequences for those who do not keep on top of their studies. It seems worth the time spent burning the midnight oil: the school is seen to take coursework very seriously and the system seems to be fair.

The challenge

Most universities operate a similar system for collecting assignments but it does present challenges:

- getting the deadlines from teachers is not easy

- some teachers do not want to trust the Senior Leadership Team to collect in work

- others feel that their own practice is being criticised

- those who are good at getting work in do not think the system should apply to them

- some are not sufficiently on top of their planning to be able to offer a specific deadline

- a few will be awkward because that is always their reaction to change

If there is not universal compliance the idea has little chance of working; it is something that needs to be insisted upon. The request has to have the force of an instruction and the responses will need to be monitored. Asking the head of year eleven to compile a list from vague responses without following up inconsistencies will lead to an incomplete list with very little authority behind it.

The whole system needs to be communicated to teachers, students and parents clearly from the outset, which will involve meetings, assemblies and letters home. It is better to do this at the outset and give people a chance to respond to the likelihood of sanctions, rather than have them react the first time one is applied. Some parents react badly, often offering weak excuses in support of their children. This will be minimised if communication is good at the outset.

The person who collects and distributes the coursework has to work from a central location and be very efficient. This is not extra work for an already busy clerk. Whoever takes it on has to have the time to treat this work as an important part of their job and respond to the flow of work as it comes in. If the administration of the task is not highly efficient, clarity is lost, students begin to sense they may get away with claiming work has been lost, and teachers lose confidence in the process. The coursework leader has to be a person with authority who is recognised by students as someone who is firm and fair. Appointing the wrong person can add to conflict and tension rather than reduce it.

Sanctions

The sanction must be applied immediately and firmly. It is always difficult to staff detentions, particularly on a nightly basis. Although the people concerned see it as important, those who commit to such an undertaking are invariably very busy and find it difficult to turn up on time, supervise the whole session and give sufficient attention to the students there to get the full benefit from the time it takes up. The easy answer is a rota of some kind, but it is difficult to ensure that everyone on it has the authority to keep students on task. The greater the number of people involved, the more opportunity there is for students to slip through the net. It has to be someone who is able to commit the time needed when it is needed every night: they have to be capable of making some of the least committed of students apply themselves to a task and be able to follow up issues such as non-attendance and failure to bring sufficient materials or work. It is wise for a member of the Senior Leadership Team to support this person by turning up during the detention and showing an interest but they are too busy, especially at that time in the day, to be able to guarantee attendance and full attention, unless they excuse themselves from meetings and dealing with parents and phone calls. It is better to find someone with the right characteristics, who can supervise meaningful work sessions and be relied upon to commit themselves to this task every night for the duration of the process. It does not have to be a qualified teacher but if it is they will need to be remunerated for their efforts in so crucial a cause and probably be given non-contact time to follow things through.

Impact and quality

This strategy will have a huge impact on the handing in of coursework but there may also be some work to do to ensure that the quality improves. Giving young people a lot of time to do the work often means that it was set weeks ahead of the deadline. For teachers this is usually sufficient because they can plan their time in such a way as to meet multiple deadlines. Most are quite good at this. Many students are also adept at planning work so that it can be drafted, checked, improved, redrafted and handed in on time but there are many who are not. Students on the borderline, particularly boys, seem to have a limited grasp on the rate at which time passes. A deadline of four weeks seems forever away. The work can be forgotten about for ages, not even appearing on the radar until it is imminent. At this point it becomes an issue of some stress that is avoided by dodging it altogether or handing in just enough work to avoid immediate unpleasantness. Such work is untidy, poorly developed and a long way short of the desired quality. This happened with the same assignments last year, the year before and the year before that. Lengthy deadlines, especially for extended writing, resemble the Titanic for many young students. When coursework is set, the ship goes sailing off in the direction of the iceberg. In a few weeks you will see the collision coming but it is too late to avoid it and the inevitable happens. The difference is that the real Titanic only sailed once. You send your metaphorical one off every year and annually mourn the consequences.

Interim deadlines

It is possible that every student would benefit from an interim deadline. This might even be fed into the central coursework submission system if there is sufficient capacity. Even if this is a duplication of effort involving many students who do not need it, a significant proportion of them would really benefit. It would be surprising if teachers couldn't sit down in September and pinpoint with considerable accuracy which students these

will be throughout year eleven. At the very least teachers should be encouraged to arrange an interim deadline for the young people who need it and get an early draft of work in, or the first few sections done. It would get students to think about the specific piece weeks before they otherwise might, and would enable teachers to see who is struggling with the piece of work and take a little of the pressure off everyone involved. It is also a good idea to photocopy the work handed in before returning it. A sizeable amount of marks are dropped by certain students for work the teacher has seen in draft but which has since been lost.

This works for a number of reasons. The chunking of work makes it manageable for students who find the whole project intimidating. It also makes it possible to offer praise and encouragement along the way. Many boys find it difficult to work towards deferred gratification and need the extra impetus that a positive word from a teacher gives from time to time along the way. It also enables teachers to look at work and offer suggestions for improvement, or offer a steer that will bring more marks in the remainder of the work.

A fair deal for all

Teachers should not offer an unprofessional amount of direction and guidance because we have a responsibility to colleagues working with young people in other schools for whom the higher GCSE grades are equally important, and we should not give the message to students that doing what is ethical is less important than success. However there are ways to make suggestions to students that get them to engage with a piece of work in a different way, and think about aspects of it that will pick up more marks. School leaders are professional enough to be able to advise teachers to offer advice on the improvement of coursework, without applying so much pressure that they feel obliged to do what they know to be wrong. In most cases teachers can be trusted to decide where to draw the line in their area, although this is not always an easy task. I have worked with colleagues who felt the need to take a unilateral stance in defence of their own standards irrespective of the clear demands of the examination board. On one occasion a teacher proudly announced that a C in his department was worth more than one in the same subject in any other school in the area because he made the students labour for days on end to produce work that met his own standards rather than those of the external assessor. He mentioned it as part of a complaint that the moderator had awarded his students' work higher marks than he had. Awarding more marks to your own candidates than is merited penalises students elsewhere but the reverse can apply, to the detriment of your own students. It is important to do what you can to ensure that the benchmarks for assessment are applied fairly according to external standards. Sending teachers to the standardisation meetings run by the examination boards is an important part of ensuring this.

Sometimes there is no standardisation of coursework grading across departments. Leaving teachers to their own discretion is poor practice. Internal standardisation discovers anomalies, offers valuable professional development and provides opportunity for teachers to discuss ways to enable students to score more highly – next year if not this.

When meeting subject leaders to help form action plans for the coming year, based upon GCSE results, it is wise to ask which assessment components the crucial students do least well in. Coursework is often cited as an area of particular weakness and when asked to develop the discussion Heads of Department state that it is missed, late or poor. At this point it is worth asking which particular pieces of work went least well, and what they were designed to assess. It is worth focusing the discussion down to the level of particular questions to see if certain problems can be identified. It is impossible to be an expert in the assessment of all subjects but it is important to encourage that level of

thought because it prompts specific changes in approach on the part of teachers. This has to be more useful than encouraging them to get in more, better work next time. It gives them a chance to demonstrate their depth of knowledge, forces them to analyse student performance more carefully and shows that you really are taking an interest in their endeavours to improve their practice.

You might ask:

- Who appeared to fall short on coursework last year?

- When was the work scheduled to be handed in?

- Who missed the deadline?

- Were particular teachers better at getting work in on time?

- How long did students have to complete it?

- Were there interim deadlines?

- Was any opportunity for professional feedback created and taken?

- Are there particular teachers who could teach the coursework element to the whole year group?

- Could work have been broken up?

Mark Schemes

When working with teachers who are trying to secure a higher proportion of A or A* grades it is often worth asking them what is it in the work of a student at A* that is different from one at A or B? I always get an answer, usually after a pause for thought, but it is often not convincing. This is less prevalent at the C boundary but it happens there too. Many teachers are not absolutely clear what the distinction is. If this is true of teachers, how can students possibly be clear what to do to secure the grade they seek? As long as sharing the mark scheme does not involve the divulging of necessary content it should be a crucial part of revision and coursework preparation. If the difference between grades C and D is extended explanation, teachers should model this skill and show how certain key words like 'because' and 'also' can automatically lead to better grades. You don't get better grades simply by writing more.

Students need to be given clear definitions of what is required for the various grades and retain them in a conspicuous place. In order to reinforce learning, examples of work can be provided for the students to mark according to a mark scheme provided for them.

> We often assume students understand the lexicon of assessment, because they don't ask about it. It is second nature to us, but do they really know what terms like analyse, evaluate, synthesise or extension mean? Do they know how to demonstrate that knowledge?

Does the preparation of coursework involve working with these terms using a mark scheme? When a young person says they could not do a piece of work because they did not understand it, they may be telling the truth, because they simply didn't understand the focus of the piece as well as they might. This approach will help all students. Did the student really know what it was they had to demonstrate to get their target grade and does the teacher know it well enough to convey it properly?

Small groups

Borderline students will not achieve their potential if they work in large groups. Several times I have asked heads of department whether they would get grade C if they were able to teach a borderline student one-to-one. The answer has been that they would: more often than not they say the student would have achieved grade B. The student clearly has the potential for B. So surely the fact that schools have to be organised in classes of 25 or 26 militates against success for some students, particularly borderline students? For this reason some schools have begun to introduce coursework to borderline students

separately and in groups of three or four. This gives them a better chance of understanding the brief and allows a closer more personal follow-up when the coursework begins. By sensible use of interim checks, appropriate and ethical educational support and guidance and an insistence that the student makes amendments within days of the discussion of the developing coursework, standards can be improved.

This makes demands on teacher time. There is a reason why classes are the size they are. Finances dictate that teachers have to be deployed with viable class sizes. Somehow ways have to be found to create time to allow some teachers to meet with students in smaller groups.

Using other students

Schools with sixth forms have a valuable resource at hand. Only a year ago students in year twelve were experiencing coursework for themselves. Why not pair students, borderline in Geography, say, with a sixth former who has achieved grade A in Geography just twelve months earlier? They can be as good as a teacher, seeing things from the student perspective and giving personal support and guidance. If you use this opportunity you need to give clear guidance to the sixth form student:

> you can discuss the coursework project with the students
>
> you can suggest sources of information
>
> you can help with internet access
>
> you can introduce useful books
>
> you can reveal what you found helpful
>
> you can read their coursework and make suggestions
>
> you cannot do the coursework for them

Many students have personal tutors who visit their homes. Borderline students often have neither the interest in nor the family support for personal tuition. Using volunteer sixth formers in this way appeals to borderline students because it is peer support and is not a drain on family finance. For the sixth form students it is an opportunity to give something back to the school community, a way to make a difference for others. Who knows? It might encourage recruits to the teaching profession! A scheme like this needs professional supervision both in the initial training of sixth formers and in monitoring the work they do, the help they give and the impact they are having.

What should be the aim?

So much time is spent on getting coursework in. Sometimes this is at the expense of quality. The aim for all borderline students should be B- or C+. When the coursework grade is added to the examination grade it often takes a C+ to compensate for a D- in the terminal examination. Settling for a C- may well leave the student short. Great care needs to be taken with individuals to ensure that if they are capable of C+ or B- they get it for the coursework.

Action points

■ Structure a series of interviews with subject heads to determine what can be done to improve coursework

■ Appoint someone to lead on coursework issues

■ Collect specific and fixed deadlines from teachers

■ Establish a central coursework submission system

■ Determine a sanction that will help solve the problem

■ Inform students and parents of the approach being taken and why

■ Create small groups of borderline students to handle coursework

■ Recruit sixth form help, train and brief them fully. Appoint a leader

■ Insist that heads of department aim high with borderline students' coursework

■ Ensure that all teachers and students have a good

Arnold Fletcher

Chapter 9

Through the curriculum

*Discover and provide the
conditions under which people's
learning curves go off the chart*
Barth

Succeeding – or failing – to meet a
challenging target for improvement at
GCSE is determined by the choice of
curriculum offered to students. Increasingly
schools are using a pathways approach, in
which various alternatives are given to
students, including vocational courses with
GCSE equivalence built in, alongside the
more traditional GCSE approach. Given that a
great deal is known about students by the
time these choices have to be made accurate
guidance can be given to students doing three
things:

- ensuring that the pathway towards
the terminal examinations at the end
of year 11 offers balance alongside
suitability

- ensuring that the courses undertaken
give students their best chance of
achieving their potential

- making sure there is an appropriate
career path after GCSE

Schools use a variety of strategies to bring this
about.

1. Choosing the right subjects
Teachers guiding students along the best
pathways have some internal information to
bear in mind. Not only do they take into
account a student's interest and aptitude but
they also consider:

- the previous record of a particular
department

Some departments in a school have a poor
record at GCSE. Students may be unaware of
this but teachers certainly are. Guidance has
to be given bearing in mind that placing a
student on a course in that subject will
considerably reduce their chances of success
at C level compared with pursuing an
alternative course where the track record is
better. In most cases, students have a final say
on such matters but shrewd guidance can
give them maximum chances with no
significant detriment.

- staffing issues

Internal intelligence reveals that some
departments are going to experience
upheaval in the next year. When you know
there is difficulty recruiting staff or the long-
term unresolved absence of a teacher,
borderline students would struggle to achieve
on a course in those departments. Other
students may struggle too, and this creates a
problem over whether to offer courses in
those subjects at all – at the risk that
disruption will damage achievement overall
or to continue with the course in the hope
that suitable cover teachers may be found.
When there is a concentration on making a

55

significant advance in results you cannot afford borderline students being put at risk in uncertain situations like these.

■ inexperienced teachers

Many schools have departments with teachers following a GCSE course for the first time. This need not be a problem but in some circumstances it can be. If both the teacher and the head of department are new there may not be clarity about what you have to do to achieve C. The teacher will understand in general terms but their compative naivety means they are less well-equipped to drive borderline students through to grade C. Experience will come, of course, but while it is being developed you will have to assess what you will do to compensate for any inadequacy. Adjustments can be made to the way the classes are taught if they have such a teacher. Extra support can be introduced or a mentor provided to offer help, but the underlying issue could lead to students under-achieving. You will need to decide whether to guide borderline students away from this situation or to compensate for it.

2. Emphasis on the core subjects

Traditionally the core subjects have been Mathematics, English, Science, Physical Education and Religious Studies. These are defined as core because they are subjects studied by almost all students. A new definition of core is evolving from developments in how league tables are published. At the moment all subjects have equal status as far as these tables are concerned. However, the government has begun to show concern about the percentage of students achieving good GCSE grades in Mathematics and English as part of their overall score of 5 or more. They appear concerned that although results are improving significantly, it may be because other subjects are being used to bring about this advance, notably multiple grade GCSEs in ICT and other vocational subjects. These are not being frowned upon but schools are encouraged to ensure that as many students as possible achieve a C grade in the new core

by the requirement for a separate table in 2006 about achievement including Mathematics and English. This requirement will concentrate your mind. Some schools have recently improved results enormously through entering many students for courses in Information Technology where they achieve 2 C grades, and sometimes 4, in just one subject. It does not take a lot to make this into 5. Some schools have added 20 per cent to their league table scores at a stroke and now appear to be doing very well indeed compared to past results. If that has happened in your school you will be concerned not to have another table that makes matters look much worse. You may want to concentrate on Mathematics and English in a different way, to minimise the difference between the two tables.

What might you do?

■ Give additional time on the curriculum to Mathematics and English in years 10 and 11

■ Increase the number of teachers allocated to groups in year 10 or 11 to create smaller group sizes

■ Add a teacher to the timetable allocation for these subjects for some of the curriculum time so she can be used for individual or small group tuition

■ Introduce after-school classes throughout years 10 or 11 for one hour a week, targeted at borderline students. This can be used as a strategy for other groups also, but in the context of GCSE improvement needs to be focused on borderlines as a minimum

■ Arrange private coaching for small groups of students in the core. Groups should be 4 or 5 for maximum benefit. These classes can be conducted by teachers from schools other than your own. Recruiting the best from elsewhere is a helpful device in some circumstances. Running such classes for 8 weeks during spring in year 11 can do a lot of good

- Identify areas for improvement for borderline students individually using teacher knowledge and trial examination scripts

3. Offer additional subjects

At a prize-giving I attended recently a substantial number of students had achieved at least a C grade in Statistics in year 10. They had done this as an integral part of their Mathematics course with no extra time. Some of these were borderline students and consequently they had at least one subject in the achievement bank before they embarked on year 11. One school has made a significant change for some students by combining Business and Communication with Business Studies, allowing the students to use the same coursework for both. In that school there were half a dozen students who would have scored 4 GCSE grades if they had not had this legitimate doubling-up to make 5.

Many schools have used GNVQ courses in vocational subjects to achieve multiple grades. As a variation on that you could enter students for DIDA (Diploma in Digital Applications) courses in year 9. This is a natural course of action if it follows the delivery of quality teaching in an appropriate time allocation in years 7, 8 and 9. It is a massive benefit to have 2 grade C qualifications by the time your students are 14.

4. Enter students early

For some students early entry in some subjects can release time for other subjects. This may not mean adding more subjects but could allow extra time for subjects where a C might be possible. Some schools have used this device to enable a student to devote more time to double award Science or even to extend double award Science into three separate sciences. Early entry has been used for many years to start advanced courses in year 11.

5. Using half grades

Religious Studies awards both a full grade and a half grade. It is not unusual for schools to enter students for half grade GCSE in year 10 on the back of one hour's teaching per week. Often borderline students do not achieve a C grade using this procedure but some do. Teachers responsible for monitoring GCSE performance need to study these results with care. The secret is to match a half grade in one subject with a half grade in another to make a whole C. Where the Religious Studies result forms one half, schools sometimes use Citizenship to form the other.

For the 5 A* to C measure half grades are useless. They may be good reward for a worthwhile course but as far as raising GCSE achievement is concerned they contribute nothing.

Archbishop Tenison School in Croydon selected a dozen boys who had a good Religious Studies result in year 10 and offered them 20 weeks of small group tuition in Religious Studies after school in year 11. The majority of them achieved a full grade C.

6. Planning a reduced curriculum

Years ago students did 9 GCSE examinations. Now the number can vary from 19 to none at all. Many schools feel that some borderline students are doing too many examinations. They do not need them all and they cannot cope with them all. The reason why they are retained on some courses is because schools don't know what they can do with them. If the student is withdrawn from an examination where will he spend the released time. The alternatives seem to be:

- stay in the class but don't do the exam

- sit at the back of the class and do some other work

- go to a supervised study room with work set by teachers of subjects that they are still taking

None of these ideas is popular. Each creates problems. If the student sits at the back of the class without doing the examination they lose interest and cause disruption. When the student is supposed to do other work he often forgets to bring it. Teachers who are supposed to set work for the student do not always do so unless you have strong supervision arrangements. And the amalgamation of several students withdrawn from various lessons all in one room can be a nightmare so most schools leave things alone. It is argued that once you allow one student to withdraw, others will want to.

There is an alternative. You can plan an alternative timetable for students who are withdrawn from lessons. Such a system should operate after trial examinations for a limited time period not exceeding six weeks. This involves:

- Careful screening of which students are to be allowed to do this

- Detailed explanation to all students of why this is planned

- Analysis of borderline students' subjects to identify which subjects can be relinquished

- Explanation to staff of the benefits to both staff and students

- Preparation of an alternative timetable for each student

- Allocation of a student to a room where the teacher has a class from a much younger age group and teaches a subject that the student needs for a portfolio of 5 GCSE

- Outlining a *modus operandi* for the system to staff, students and parents

- Appointing an overseer of the procedure

- Defining a reward and incentive system to encourage compliance

- Communication with parents about the features and benefits of the plan

The schools that have invested in Revision Guides may find these useful now. The *modus operandi* could include:

a *proforma* to be taken to every scheduled alternative lesson requiring a signature from the teacher evaluating

Student present ☐

Student on task without supervision ☐

Student produced good work ☐

Student arrived on time ☐

It needs to be simple but relevant. The teacher takes the *proforma* from the student and hands it to the overseer of the programme. They are collected by the overseer and incentives are given for those students using the procedure well. If you have about 20 students involved with this system, it is constructive and educational if a team of five of the 20 make the awards to the winners according to criteria set out by the overseer. If awards are made fortnightly there is space for three different teams to have an opportunity to be the awards' jury. There is considerable learning for students when they do this and it helps them to develop a consciousness of good practice. Examples of an amended timetable are shown in the appendices.

Action points

- Take a close look at the results of GCSE examinations comparing and contrasting departmental performance

- Formulate a policy about how this will impact on guidance to students

- Decide whether any teachers engaged with year 11 classes could damage the student's chances. Decide what to do about it.

- Senior leaders decide if there should be an early entry policy: if so in what subjects? Develop a curriculum model for discussion.

- Decide whether students should be released from some subjects and at what stage of the course.

- Formulate a rigorous plan to handle this situation

Chapter 10

Through subject leaders

It's skill not strength that governs a ship

Thomas Fuller

A leader must know, must know that they know, and make it abundantly clear to others that they know

Clarence Randall

There are two strands to transforming GCSE performance. The first, motivation, is the subject of an earlier chapter, and there is an equal need to impact on performance in the subjects a student is being taught. The responsibility for this falls upon either the head of faculty or the head of department. John Gardner observed that *most ailing organisations have developed a functional blindness to their own defects. They are not suffering because they cannot resolve their problems, but because they cannot see them.* If we interpret the possibility that about 10 per cent might be added to your GCSE score as a sign of 'ailing' it may well be happening without many leaders of subjects seeing any problem. It is not, as Gardner says, that they cannot resolve the problem, rather that they cannot see it.

Kotter (2002) believes that the first step in achieving transformation is to have a sense of urgency about the need to make the change. If you do not see the need there can be no sense of urgency. The leaders of a school have

to address this matter. How senior leaders deal with middle or subject leaders, as we will call heads of faculty or heads of department, is clearly fundamental to making the changes you want to see. How can this be handled?

The importance of middle leaders

It is only recently that these people have been called middle leaders. Formerly they were known as middle managers. It is a significant change, clear in the mind of senior leaders without filtering down into the minds of the middle leaders themselves. These people often feel devalued, sometimes ridiculed. And not without good cause. Sir Nick Scheele of Ford said of middle leaders in the motor industry:

> *It is common in internal corporate communication to erode morale without intending to. The scapegoating of middle managers is a case in point. In Ford, I found that they were referred to as 'the layer of clay'. How motivated and energised would you feel if you knew that's the kind of language the people at the top were using to refer to you?*

It is not a phenomenon peculiar to the motor industry. You will not get the best out of middle leaders if their morale is low. These are significant people in the delivery of results in any school. They are hugely influential on teachers and students. To add 10 per cent to your GCSE results will require a lot of middle leaders to improve what they deliver. They are not likely to do so unless they are handled wisely and well.

Responsibility to middle leaders

Last year I worked with a fine headteacher. We had talked for a couple of hours and the conversation was drawing to a close. I asked him casually what he was doing for the rest of the afternoon.

> *'I am going to bollock the Head of ICT,'* he replied.

> *'Oh, why is that?'* I said.

> *'His results were awful,'* he responded.

There was a moment of quietness. He clearly thought that justified his action and I did not know whether I should say what I thought. I did.

> *'I wouldn't do that,'* I said.

> *'Why not? His results were awful,'*

> *'Maybe it was your fault as much as his. Were the results a shock to you? Had you no idea this was going to happen? Had you checked how things were during the course of the year?'*

We did not discuss it much more but I know he reflected on what was said to him. The trouble is that often these middle leaders are simply left to it. Some of them like that and deliver well; some like it but don't deliver at all well. Leaving people to it, not knowing what they are doing or why, not being aware of how things are developing is not good practice, even if it is common. You need to take responsibility for what the middle leaders are achieving and give serious thought to what you can do as senior leaders to help them in their work.

The challenge to middle leaders needs to be specific and personal

One obvious place where all this can be focused is in the meeting between senior leaders and middle leaders when examination results are reviewed. These meetings generally take place in September. Their effectiveness varies enormously. If you take the challenge to raise results by around 10 per cent seriously, this is a good place to start. You might ask:

> Which of your students did not quite achieve grade C?

> What was each one's prior attainment?

> Did these students show an uneven pattern of performance across the teachers in your department?

> How did these students' results in your subject compare to their other subjects?

There are many sophisticated statistical ways to look at evidence. One useful way is to draw up a table for all students in your subject scoring each student as

> +2 if your subject grade was their SINGLE highest grade

> +1 if your subject as their EQUAL highest grade

> 0 if your subject was none of the other four

> -1 if your subject was their EQUAL worst grade

> -2 if your subject as their SINGLE worst grade.

This has proved to be useful because:

- ■ it is straightforward

English	+2	+1	0	-1	-2
Miss Shah	3	14	8	2	0
Mr Bertolli	0	1	14	10	2

figure 6

- it compares each subject against others for the same student

- it reveals trends in class groups

In figure 6 there are some hypothetical figures for two teachers.

It is glaringly obvious in this example that one teacher is doing significantly better than the other. It may mean nothing. There may be explanations but the questions need asking. The middle leader needs to be asked but so do the individual teachers. Middle leaders are not good at doing this.

By far the best way is to devise a system for middle leaders to use to analyse their own results and invite them to present their findings. Congratulations and celebrations over conspicuous success are warranted but it is also important to ask probing questions. The process of transformation can then begin.

Some headteachers send an analysis of the examination results through the post to each subject leader directly the results are published, along with a series of questions for their consideration. This gives weight to the follow-up and focuses the agenda well. Too often the review happens so long after the results are published that it loses much of its impact. With early distribution of results and analysis papers, there is the possibility of review very early in September.

Four steps in creating a challenge for middle leaders can lead to transformation

- *appreciate – what is*

Using carefully analysed data, establish agreement on the conspicuous successes. Do not rush past this to the issues you think really matter! Over-ambitious parents do it with their children: they read the glowing report, overlook all that is good and focus on any hints of weakness. It is a mistake to by-pass success to focus on weakness. Before dealing with 'issues that really matter', begin with appropriate celebration of what is good. It is crucial to investigate what made these

features good. Unless leaders know why they achieved what they did they are unlikely to be able to repeat it.

- *envision – what might be*

Unless you can get agreement with middle leaders on an attractive outcome they would like to achieve, significant change is unlikely. You need to start with the moral high ground and appeal to the inner conviction of most teachers that they want the best for the students. They want to make a difference. They want students and their families to celebrate success in their subject and the middle leaders want their team to feel as though it has done really well by all its students. Many student leaders do indeed feel like that, a lot pretend to, some reckon they have done well when they have not, and some know they could do more if a way could be found. Occasionally one encounters a middle leader who lives in a different world. I met one who refused to 'water down mathematics', as he put it – 'we should be preparing people for A level maths!' All this in a school with less than 30 per cent of its students achieving grade C. This teacher would not do Modular Mathematics on principle. Such situations are mercifully rare.

- *dialogue – what should be*

Dialogue is fundamentally different from either debate or discussion. Peter Senge (1990) points out that the word discussion comes from the same route as percussion and concussion, and can often be the equivalent of knocking the other person over the head with your ideas. David Bohm (1996) argues that in dialogue we are engaged in collective new thinking, not exchanging pre-cooked thoughts.

Senior leaders need to have some ideas not only on what they would like to see but also about how to make it happen. Middle leaders are weary of targets. Telling them that 'We expect this or that' is of little use without offering ideas on how to achieve this or that. People are suffering from target fatigue. This book could encourage another target -'add 10 per cent to GCSE'. That would be outrageous were some ways not proposed on how to do it. It is fair to assume that most people are doing all they can to achieve well and just do not know what more to do. Since I began consultancy work I have met some wonderful people who were doing all they could think of, working very hard and sometimes fretting at their inability to break through the glass ceiling of the performance of the school. They were innovative in many other areas of school life but found difficulty raising standards. They were wide open to new ideas, no 'know it all' attitudes. 'Don't just give us another target, give us some new ideas or point us in the direction of where they are.'

So we all need to look inside education or outside it for new ideas, to people with similar problems who have found new solutions. We need to have a picture of what should be. Senior leaders have a key role in helping their middle leaders to find these people and these solutions. Some ideas in these pages have brought new life and new hope to struggling leaders, both senior and middle leaders, so that they not only see what should be but have some idea how to do it.

■ *create the personalised vision – what will be*

There are three stages in starting motivational work with students. The first is to get them to say with confidence *I can*. Too often middle ability students have no confidence – they do not believe they *can* actually achieve 5 A* to C grades. The second stage is to get them to say *I want to*. If you do not believe you can there is no way you will want to. But some people believe they can do something but still have no desire or aspiration. The final step is to get students to say *I will*. I know now that I can and I want to so I will. If you can move through those three stages you have a chance of making change with students and with middle leaders too. I can move my results up by x per cent and I really want to. So I will make the effort, I will investigate ideas, I will formulate a plan. If it does not happen it will not be because I would not do it. Creating

that personal vision is not easy work. It will require quality time set aside for talking between senior and middle leaders, individually and in groups, it will need a re-focusing on moral purpose and it will mean accumulating ideas that work and sharing them together.

Focus on students

How different would things in our school be if we viewed students as our customers? Too often they are faced with a take it or leave it attitude from a school. 'This is what we offer and that's it'. Little attention is given to whether it is what the client wants, what counts is what schools think they need. John Russell explained the attitude at Harley-Davison: *we don't create loyalty. Our customers give us their loyalty. They choose to show that they believe in us and in the way we run our business and processes.* No wonder Harley-Davison remains a unique brand and world leader. If schools treated students as clients in the same way they might question why their students are unmotivated by what they offer, not giving their loyalty, much attention, co-operation or enthusiasm. The students may not be to blame; it might be what the school is doing.

The best middle leaders address these questions. They should all do so. And if you want to find out what the customers think, you ask them, but in a way that allows them to say what they honestly think. You *take notice* of what they say. You look at the hard evidence and apply some honest thinking to discerning what is behind the brutal facts. You say to middle leaders 'this is not your problem, it is *our* problem, now what can we do about it.' You want people to achieve who are not achieving. Some creative thinking is going to be necessary. What can a teacher do in her subject to obtain student commitment from those reluctant to give it? How can we work together to get the most out of those who will not achieve C unless something different is done? Not even Harley-Davison will fully satisfy everybody. Nor will you. But the client focused approach of many successful businesses offers schools some approaches that will prove successful.

Don't allow incrementalism

Many middle leaders are happy to improve GCSE performance by any percentage no matter how small. If a school is aiming to raise achievement by a significant percentage because it believes it is possible then many middle leaders, if not all, need to see that they need to do it too. The contrast between incremental thinking and radical thinking is shown below:

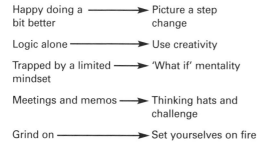

Conservative middle leaders operate on the left hand side of this model. They rationalise, analyse and explain performance. They justify what they do on the grounds that the students are achieving as well as they can. They are organised and meticulous in planning lessons that are ordered, systematic and routine, though often lacking in vitality,

challenge, flair and dynamism, and the team works hard, so hard that they may be worn out. It feels like a daily grind. The department achieves sound but not startling results. Students are prepared for examinations but not inspired. Results oscillate around the same percentage year on year depending on the vagaries of the marking system. Too many departments are held back by the fear of aiming too high.

The middle leaders in transformational departments have a different attitude. They can see that step change might be possible though not easy. They argue that '*we will keep getting what we always got*' if we keep doing '*what we have always done*'. They find ways to think outside the box. They create time to ask '*how can we make this situation change?*' They are risk-takers. They ask '*what if we did this or that?*' They want to escape from the routines that make them into rut dwellers and devise tactics to break out of the mould. They recognise that fire within is likely to produce more energy than grinding on and will elicit more response. They take up the challenge and enjoy the fight to reach the heights. They need encouragement and support from their leaders whether they hit the targets first time or not. These people are invaluable in a

Student	Form			Prior Attainment
David Smith	11ZA			455

Subject	Present	Predicted	Potential	Teacher
Maths	E	D	C	Mrs Wilson
English	D	C	C	Mr Keith
Literature	D	D	C	Mr Keith
Science	DD	DD	CC	Miss Alam
History	C	B	B	Ms Hyatt
French	E	D	D	Mme Charaud
ICT	CC	BB	BB	Miss Dover
Design Graphics	E	D	DD	Mr Frazer
Total	3	4	8	

figure 7

school trying to lift results significantly. It is easy for senior leaders to value staff of this kind and write others off. This is not wise. By careful planning, training, support and emphasising and modelling a risk-taking culture, people can be encouraged to move from left towards right. De Bono (1999) introduced the concept of six thinking hats, a device to insist that people focus on different thinking strategies one at a time. He argued that creative thinking is often sunk by cautious negative thinking and that it is important to make space for creative thinking without that danger.

Middle leaders can be helped in the following ways:

1. Data should be prepared for middle leaders by senior leaders

A list of key marginal or borderline students will be available in school. Recommendations on how this is prepared were identified in chapter 5. It is helpful to set the list out in the format shown on page 63.

Present means the teacher assessment of the grade the student would achieve if he maintained his present level through to the examination. Trial examination results are sometimes used to determine this grade.

Predicted is the grade the teacher believes the student will get if she improves as students often do over the course of the year. Sometimes schools use external prior data to determine this grade and call it Prior rather than Predicted.

Potential grade is the grade the teacher believes the student is capable of on the basis of personal judgement and previous professional experience.

Prior attainment in the top corner of figure 7 shows the scores by some national assessment measure. These are scores in Key Stage 3 tests in Maths, English and Science. In general terms any students with a total of 15 or more ought in most circumstances to achieve at least 5 A* to C grades. The score in English is particularly significant. A five here offers hope in many subject areas. Students

scoring 13 or 14 often also achieve 5 A* to C. They should not be written off, though they present a greater challenge.

You can see that a student like David Smith is a borderline student defined in terms of 5 A* to C grades. On present form he will achieve 3, is predicted to achieve 4 but has potential to achieve 8. He is worth special attention.

Closer analysis of figure 7 shows that some subjects appear to be strong. These are green.

Some are marginal and these are yellow and the remainder are unlikely to yield C or better and will be called red. Green subjects are English, History and ICT because all assessments for the later stages are positively indicating C or better. Yellow subjects retain some uncertainty about them. These are Maths, Literature and Science. The 'no-hope' subjects, reds, are French and Design Graphics. These subjects are not regarded as unimportant but, *in terms of the achievement of 5 or more C plus grades*, they are going to play no part. The amount of extra time dedicated to them should therefore be minimal. A composite sample is shown in the appendices and the format is on the CD.

2. Assemble results in departmental groups

For every student in the borderline group you will have a set of data like that shown in figure 7. These can be produced on a huge spreadsheet to be easily seen. From this list extract all students who are green or yellow by subject. A hypothetical example is shown in figure 8 for Mathematics, where the teacher is shown by their initials in column six.

This list is given to the Head of Mathematics (initials AVF) at a meeting arranged with the headteacher who explains that school data shows that the students shown need Mathematics to secure at least 5 GCSE results at C or better. These students are not more important than any others but in the context of the aims of the school their success is essential if the aims are to be achieved. What can AVF do to ensure that this happens? No

Mathematics

Student	Form	Present	Predicted	Potential	Teacher	Colour
Ahmed	11ZA	E	D	C	JAK	Yellow
Backer	11KD	D	D	C	MGY	Yellow
Dashton	11 ZF	D	C	C	RT	Green
Davies	11 KB	D	C	B	MGY	Green
Fullan	11 ZE	E	C	C	AVF	Green
Hutton	11KC	E	D	C	RT	Yellow
Khan	11ZF	D	B	B	JAK	Green
Miller	11 KA	D	D	C	AVF	Yellow
Reina	11 ZC	E	D	C	MGY	Yellow
Starr	11 KB	D	C	B	RT	Green
Sterling	11 ZE	D	C	C	MGY	Green
Thomas	11 KA	E	E	C	RT	Yellow
Uzziam	11 ZE	D	D	C	AVF	Yellow
Zhalid	11 KB	E	C	C	JAK	Yellow

figure 8

doubt AVF will have some ideas. It is as well if the headteacher has some too. The headteacher will make AVF aware that he has autonomy to make this happen with the full support of the headteacher, and agreement needs to be reached on the percentage of these students who will get the required C. This becomes the aim for AVF, who must produce a detailed action plan of how to achieve this aim within a fortnight of the meeting.

In this example you can see that AVF teaches three students on the list, RT teaches four, JAK teaches three and MGY four. AVF will know what he intends to do about his three students but the plan must identify what the other teachers are going to do about this and what the accountability procedures will be.

3. Insist on the borderline students being treated differently

These students need to be made to feel special. We make a habit of telling them they are but that is not how it feels for many of them. Feeling hidden amongst the mediocre masses does not feel special. Generally schools arrange activities to help borderline students such as revision classes and coursework catch up. Often, for logistical reasons, they are lumped together with other more able students. This is regularly the case in after-school revision classes. It is ineffective. Reasons for this are discussed in detail in later chapters. For best results treat these students differently and separately: after all there are only fourteen of them in this example. In most schools it is not a huge group for any subject. They need personal attention because it is more difficult to turn yellow into green without it.

David Hopkins, until 2005 the chief adviser on school standards at the DfES, asked in a lecture, 'Why can't every school be great?' He suggested five key drivers to make this happen:

- Personalising learning – tailoring teaching and learning to enable every student to reach their potential

- Informed professionalism – using data and evidence to apply a rich repertoire of pedagogic strategies to meet students' needs

- Segmentation – a highly differentiated approach to school improvement

- Networks and extended schooling – networks to build diversity and specialisms and create high expectations

- Intelligent accountability – self-evaluation and 'bottom up' target setting

This system exemplifies Hopkins' personalised approach, based on informed professionalism. It specifically involves some in-school segmentation so that a differentiated approach will result in improvement in school performance. In London and elsewhere schools are working in partnerships or networks to create high expectations and develop practical ways of fulfilling them.

4. Issue list to each teacher

The Head of Department will be expected to disaggregate the list, see figure 8, and distribute a smaller list to each member of staff involved, see figure 9.

The Head of Department will meet each teacher and discuss what is to be done to ensure that these borderline students improve their grades to achieve their potential. The challenge is to turn yellow to green. Just as you would not expect a Head of Department to achieve 100 per cent of the target set, so you ought not to demand that of the teacher either. In the case of JAK you may set a target of at least 2 of the 3 in her class. Clearly an explanation of the colouring system will be necessary. Strategies she might use to bring about this improvement are shown in the next chapter.

5. An Action Plan is produced

To ensure that the vision becomes reality most people will have to create a detailed action plan. It will need scheduled meetings, support strategies and accountability systems built into it. An example follows. The dates are hypothetical and the detail extreme but the concept is well-illustrated. We call this form AOPE: Aims (where we will be by when), Objectives (the steps on the way to getting there), Purpose (why we are doing this). This Purpose section is best when the purpose specified is Moral Purpose as opposed to Pragmatic Purpose because more energy is created by the one than the other. Little energy is generated when people do something because they are told to (which is often the pragmatic purpose). The final section is Evaluation (the measure of whether you have done what you said you would do in the Objective section, hence the same number in each section). Here is the example of the Action Plan:

AIMS

To ensure that 80 per cent of the key marginal students in this department achieve at least C in the final GCSE (we have 14 of which we need at least 12 to get C+).

NB I will make this clear to all my staff by November 1, 2006

For JAK						
Student	**Form**	**Present**	**Predicted**	**Potential**	**Teacher**	**Colour**
Ahmed	11ZA	E	D	C	JAK	Yellow
Khan	11ZF	D	B	B	JAK	Green
Zhalid	11 KB	E	C	C	JAK	Yellow

figure 9

OBJECTIVES (dates are hypothetical)

1. Receive list from Deputy headteacher of who these students are by Nov 7

2. Publish this list for all the department by Nov 12

3. Hold departmental meeting to discuss ways in which we can influence these students before Nov 21

4. List all ideas submitted by the team after this meeting by Nov 25

5. Require each teacher to prepare an AOPE for each key marginal student in their class by Dec 2

6. Go through each AOPE with each class teacher by December 10

7. Pass on amended AOPEs following discussion to DHT by Dec 17

8. Discuss progress at departmental meeting in early January

9. Meet each class teacher to receive report on each key marginal in their class by Jan 31

10. Provide extra classes for this group in batches of 4 for 8 weeks of 1 hour from February 3

11. Check these students' trial exam results by February 15

12. Meet each class teacher to receive report on each key marginal in their class by February 28

13. Meet students one by one who are making real progress to reward and commend by March 5

14. Make suggestions to teachers on what else might be done for those not progressing by March 10

15. Hold departmental review for further ideas by March 31

16. Give all these students a second trial exam by April 10

17. Review outcomes with class teacher and introduce further incentives for those still on borderlines by April 20

18. Offer specific guidance to these students in pairs so that their coursework reaches C+ / B- if that is possible by February 27

19. Plan prepared on what to do on exam day for these students and meet all these students on the day of the exam to encourage, support and motivate

PURPOSE

■ To help young people obtain a GCSE which will be useful for their future

■ To play our part in helping students get 5 GCSEs so they can truly celebrate and feel good

■ To feel as though we are making a big difference for young people

■ To enable our department to contribute fully to what our school is achieving

■ To help our school be held in high esteem in this community

EVALUATION

1. List available from me if requested by Nov 8

2. List on boards in department on Nov 13

3. Minutes of departmental meeting available after Nov 22

4. Ideas discussed in written form for DHT by Nov 26

5. Action plans from all teachers in my hand by Dec 4

6. Minutes of meetings with each teacher on file by Dec 11

7. Amended AOPEs with DHT by Dec 19

8. Minutes of departmental meeting in early Jan

9. Notes from meeting with teachers available by Feb 2

10. Extra classes began on Feb 3 (or within five days from then)

11. Trial exam results in the department files by Feb 16

12. Minutes of meetings held with class teacher by March 2

13. Schedule of meetings and reports with letters to parents on file by March 8

14. List of new recommendations for what we might do are on staff board in department by March 11

15. Minutes of departmental meeting where review was conducted to DHT by Apr 2

16. Trial exam held and results in department by April 15

17. Individual analysis of results with class teacher and new Action Plan by Apr 25

18. Coursework moderated by an external adviser and confirmed at C+/B- by March 10

19. Plan published to department of what we will do on exam day with notes added on how it worked out

In the consultancy work I do, I often request action plans. Recently I received a fine plan that began with two aims. The first was fine. It said:

Identify 25 borderline students to be monitored using data by October 25.

The second one said:

Ensure that coursework is completed to the best of the student's ability.

I questioned whether this was specific enough. I asked the school leader why he had not developed the first one. Why not write:

60 per cent of the 25 identified students to achieve 5 A* to C in GCSE next summer

or, if coursework is to be the focus:

80 per cent of the 25 identified students to achieve C+ / B- for their coursework in marginal subjects.

The percentages don't matter, they are a matter for the school, but the specific aim is important. Vague aims often lead to average results.

6. Introduce practical accountability

Accountability is not the strongest skill in the educational world. But for effective transformation it is necessary. It need not be heavy-handed or oppressive. It can be handled with sensitivity but must retain a hard edge. All involved need to know why there are lines of accountability and how they will be used to positive effect. Accountability, requiring teachers to explain what they have done and how, is critical for six reasons:

- It demonstrates personal interest in the work of subject leaders

- It enables the leader to praise and celebrate good practice and worthy endeavour

- It enables the leader to ask probing questions to ensure the right progress is being made and the right actions taken

- It enables the leader to advise, assist, support and redirect when necessary to reach goals

- It enables the leader to intercept activities that are not working and make alternative arrangements

- It keeps the leader aware of evidence of progress.

It is important to trust staff but not to leave staff on trust. It is not inconsistent to say that you trust people but that you want to check out the reality of a situation. After all, so much investment must not be wasted through lack of rigorous checking.

Lines of accountability should be clear and rigorous. It is common for schools to use different leaders to hold departmental heads to account by splitting the departments between members of the leadership team. If this leads to an application of different standards it will cause frustration and confusion. It is best to consider one person taking responsibility for the raising standards agenda for all departments.

7. Identify the weak points and have strategies to handle them

The middle leader is the keeper of the performance. She has to be aware of the weak areas. In the context of performance of borderline students within specific teachers' classes there are three:

- a poor teacher
- an inexperienced teacher
- a resistant teacher

A teacher may be *poor* at achieving the best grades with borderline students. There are some teachers who can be relied on to get the best out of students like this and others you would prefer did not teach these students. However, whatever their general qualities, the poor teacher's influence on key students must not be allowed to affect their chances detrimentally. Intervention may be avoided by the middle leader. 'There is nothing I can do,' she says, 'they have to teach somewhere.' This appeal to complex logistics is not good enough. It says 'let the student underachieve because I can't think of a way to address it'. A way has to be found, otherwise you contribute to the failure of the vision you agreed to. What can the leader do?

- students could switch lessons for some of their time in a way that need not embarrass any teacher
- some lessons could be team taught to ensure that these borderline students are receiving quality input at key times
- a small class can be created for a lesson or so per week with a 'free' teacher to work on specific subjects

A team of middle leaders meeting with the headteacher will soon rattle off various creative strategies if they are given quality time to think of them.

Some teachers are not poor, merely *inexperienced*. They are not fully conversant with exactly what you do to get students a C. They may be working with examination groups for the first time and the middle leader must realise that this inexperience may work against the vision and plan accordingly. This can be done through training about what exactly you need to do to get grade C, which is good personal development for the future, by checking the grades awarded for coursework or by team teaching for revision purposes.

Resistant teachers are the most difficult. Their reasons will no doubt justify the resistance and they should be heard patiently and politely. However, there is a bottom line. All teachers are charged with drawing the best potential out of young people and resistance to this must not be allowed. Reasonable arguments require reasonable responses. More resources or more time may be needed but you will never make the big leap if you do not address issues that stop you making it.

Middle leaders have a crucial role in ensuring that teachers in their team play their part in bringing about the fulfilment of the exciting vision. It is a challenging but rewarding responsibility.

There is great skill in good leadership. Arrogance is not an admirable quality in subject leaders but it is vital that they know how to make a difference with borderline students and to know that they know. This is no time for whistling in the dark. A school leader's job is to help them to know, to share ideas to develop confidence, to support and encourage, to keep on task with the vision always in sight and to support until the goal is achieved.

Action points

- Check how well you reinforce the morale of middle leaders

- Devise a simple system for analysing GCSE performance covering departments and individual teachers

- Insist on a common approach by all departments

- Decide to issue results and first analysis soon after results are published

- Enter into dialogue with the intention to create new ideas together

- Create a comprehensive list of detail about borderline students, including their subjects, grade predictions and teachers

- Analyse the grades with care categorising them green, yellow or red

- Issue all heads of department with a list of students in their department who need to get C in that subject

- Require from them an action plan on what will be done

- Arrange a meeting to discuss the plan, make suggestions and require amendments

- Plan regular review, encouragement and accountability meetings

- Ensure that lines of accountability are clear and rigorous

Arnold Fletcher

Chapter 11

Through classroom teachers

New ideas do not happen by osmosis. They come from facing ideas that challenge the familiar way of viewing things
Earl and Katz (2002)

The front line service is provided by the subject teacher. Each subject teacher has a substantial group of students to look after but to shift performance at GCSE level in the way we are considering, the results of two or three students are more significant than others. All students should receive good teaching and preparation for final examinations. But there are students more at risk of failing to achieve C grades.

A system like the one suggested here ensures the subject leader knows who these students are. She will make these names known to the subject teacher so that a dialogue can take place about what the teacher can do to increase the student's chances of reaching grade C. During the meeting the subject leader should discuss possible strategies that can be employed to achieve a target of 80 per cent of the students on that teacher's list achieving grade C. The action plan (AOPE) the teacher will prepare might look as follows:

Aim:
To ensure that 80 per cent of the five key marginal students in my class achieve at least C in the final GCSE in August 2006

Objectives:

1. Receive list of borderline students in my class from subject leader by January 28

2. Prepare a personalised programme for each of these five by Feb 5

3. Put pictures of these five in my mark book and locker by February 7

4. Show my proposal to subject leader by February 8

5. Discuss and make amendments by February 15

6. Meet each of the five and outline the support I will offer by February 25

7. Go through each student's coursework with all five present at 3.30 pm on March 1

8. Give each student a week to make amendments following this meeting, to be in to me by March 8

9. Informally assess redrafted coursework and check grade with subject leader by March 14

10. Identify each student's weaknesses using previous work and trial exam by March 15

11. Report on each to subject leader with the Personalised Learning Checklist by March 20

12. Write personal letter to parents about revision session and hold revision sessions for the whole group each Thursday at 5-6 pm for 8 weeks until May 18

13. Prepare a second trial exam for these five (and the fifteen in other classes than mine) for April 12

14. Report grades on this examination to subject leader by April 16

15. Go over this paper in detail with my group, split into two subsets, giving them further help on revealed weaknesses by April 28

16. Prepare list of likely questions on GCSE exams and give students some draft answers as exemplars by May 3

17. Require each student to do two full sets of papers which I will mark and grade during mid April to mid May

18. Meet these students on the morning of the exams to encourage and offer final advice

19. Check results for my students, especially these five, and report these to subject leader on Aug 26

Purpose:

To help young people in my class to obtain a GCSE which will be so important in their future

To play my part in helping students get 5 GCSEs so they can truly celebrate and feel very good

To feel as though I am making a big difference for young people in my class

To enable our department to contribute fully to what our school is achieving

To enable our school to be held in high esteem in this community

Evaluation:

1. List available from me if requested by January 29 (see Objective 1 above)

2. Personalised programme given to subject leader by Feb 8

3. Pictures available to be seen by subject leader or headteacher by Feb 10!

4. Subject leader has my proposals by Feb 8

5. Minutes of meeting with subject leader on file by Feb 15

6. Minutes of meetings with each student on file by Feb 28

7. Make notes of meeting about coursework with my suggestions recorded by March 3

8. All revised coursework in for marking by March 9

9. Marks recorded and notes from meeting with subject leader on file by March 16

10. Listed areas of concern for each student given to subject leader and on file by March 20

11. Record of meeting with subject leader about each student's current position regarding the plan on file by March 22

12. Revision sessions in place with a personal letter to all five sets of parents by April 1

13. Exam paper prepared and given to subject leader by April 16

14. Grades available and given to subject leader and headteacher by April 20

15. Meeting was arranged and notes given to all students on file by May 1

16. Likely exam questions and exemplar answers given to subject leader by May 5

17. Two exam papers' grades given to subject leader for each student by May 15

18. Meeting with students before each exam arranged and indicated in a letter to them by May 15

19. Celebration organised to mark the results by Aug 31!

This example is guided by the following principles and practices:

1. Know exactly who the focus group is and treat them differently

The teacher knows which students are vulnerable and, more than that, whether they are likely to just make C, green, or in danger of falling short of C, yellow. No longer will these students just be one of thirty – now they are one of three, four or five. They have a higher priority because they are inextricably linked to the vision of achieving better results for them and for the school. Their needs will be looked at *individually*, no longer as part of the class. Their picture will be placed inside your locker, or in your mark book or diary, so that their image constantly reminds you of what you are trying to do. Pictures are powerful things. Rudolph Guiliani (2002) tells how his best friend Terry Hatton, chief of the New York Fire Service at the time of the September 11 horror, kept a photograph on the inside door of his locker of him rescuing a boy from a blazing building, so he never forgot what he was about. Such images remind us of our moral purpose and, at the same time, the need to focus.

2. Recognise and value accountability and support

Traditionally, teachers have retained considerable independence. They control their own classes and stand or fall by how they handle the students. This focused way of operating does not affect the independence that teachers have. Rather, it recognises that their line manager needs to know what is happening and to offer appropriate support, advice and guidance. It should not be regarded as interference in personal professional matters. Instead it is an acknowledgement that you are *together* attempting something quite significant and need to be mutually involved in its accomplishment. So it is good for them to prepare a plan of action, share it and be open to suggestions or additions likely to enhance their own ideas. It also provides opportunities to communicate problems, pressures and concerns.

3. Communicate with students and involve them fully in planning

The students need to know that maximum help is being offered. It is not that work is being done for them but that in partnership yellow can be converted into green. They should be informed of the teacher's ideas and be invited to propose ideas of their own. They need to know that their teacher is interested in them and that this interest is operating at a more personal level to address areas of underperformance so that they can reach their goal. Some students will not respond well to one-to-one developmental work and should be paired with others who feel the same.

4. Tackle coursework

Any students failing to achieve a grade C in *coursework* is unlikely to reach that target overall. Coursework offers students the opportunity to study and prepare over a substantial period of time but often borderline students do not take advantage of this. The subject teacher is in a good position to address this issue. Once again, the borderline students need to be treated differently. Too often they are lumped together with all the students and given general guidance. They are already offered more time per lesson than other students but this extra time amounts to four minutes each as opposed to two. It is not enough for students of this type. Some of these students are borderline because they need slower, more careful explanation of topics than their more able peers. Nothing unethical is being proposed. Rather teachers should ensure that students are given all the guidance that is legitimate and checks made that learning has taken place, but this needs more time than schools can manage. These students are likely to need regular meetings with teachers, either on their own or with one other student, with the coursework broken down into stages and progress reported back at regular intervals. Unlike some students in the leafy suburbs, borderline students often come from backgrounds where parents can't or won't offer support or help. They do what they do on their own. They can't access books or the internet at home; they have no private tutor to offer advice and guidance. They depend on their teacher. They need all the help they are permitted. Other ideas are discussed in the chapter Through Coursework.

5. Prepare a Personalised Learning Checklist

When teachers are asked what exactly a borderline student needs to improve to achieve grade C, the answers are often vague and imprecise. Turning yellow to green requires the teacher to know the parts of the course where the weakness is. For borderline students the reality is that there are parts of the course on which they are already secure (we call these parts green too), parts where with further support and explanation they might become secure, though they are not at the moment (we call these yellow), and parts which these students will never be able to master no matter how much help they get (we call these red). Teachers need to assess which parts of their courses have which colour for each student. A *proforma* like the hypothetical one shown for mathematics in figure 10 can be used.

The categories must be precise. Too much energy is expended on general improvement instead of focused targeted intervention. Revision classes are a classic example. With the best of intentions, the teacher offers after-school revision and packs as many anxious volunteers as possible into the room. Because anxiety hits students of all abilities, the students in the room are of all abilities: those who think they might convert B to A join with some whose present level is mid-D but who might just make C. Their needs are very different. The teacher revises many topics. For each topic covered, half could do it already, a quarter will never be able to do it and the rest might learn something. This is not an effective use of time. It emphasises teaching not learning. Often the teacher performs magnificently but no check is made on what any individual has actually learned. The Personalised Learning Checklist means that a teacher can work with a group of two, three or four students at most to focus on yellow areas they have in common: this way, far more learning will take place.

It is easy to check that it has. This is not more work – it just means doing less of one sort of class and focusing on activity that can make the biggest impact.

6. Involve parents

Part of the hypothetical plan was to contact parents. This needs to be more personal than the regular 'Dear Parent' letters. It should be addressed specifically to each family by name and be a personal letter with elements in it that clearly only apply to that family. They

G = green Y= yellow R = red	Decimals	Fractions	Percentages	Area / Volume	Substitution	Equations	Simultaneous Equations	Vectors	Angles of Triangle	Parallel Lines	Pie Graphs
Sean Adams	G	G	Y	G	G	G	R	R	Y	Y	Y
Allam Hussain	G	G	G	Y	G	Y	Y	G	G	Y	Y
Selina Mercer	Y	Y	Y	G	G	G	G	Y	G	G	Y
George Bradley	Y	G	G	G	Y	R	R	Y	G	G	Y

figure 10

need to feel that their child is being treated as an individual. The letter should explain what the teacher is doing and why, and the partnership you are establishing to bring joy and accomplishment to the student and their family. It needs to tell them that there are plans to help them reach the goal and to request their support. Different teachers will require different degrees of support. Some teachers would only ask for encouragement from parents rather than active intervention. Whatever you would like from parents needs to be made plain and they need to be fully aware what in this scheme will benefit them.

7. Consider a second examination

A Head of PE observed that several of the students he was hoping would achieve grade C had never done so before in a serious examination. This is often true of borderline students. The mock or trial exams produced D or E. Occasionally teachers contrive such results to give the students 'a shock' so they will 'wake up'. But this means many borderline students enter the examination room never having passed the subject. That must feel bad. Some schools in London have introduced second mocks conducted for certain students only. These additional examinations follow intensive preparation work to change yellow elements of the course to green and are held near to the real examination time. The Head of PE reported that a significant number of students did very well second time round and so would enter their real examination with renewed confidence. This must help. How many of you would run a marathon when your only previous experiences had been sitting on the roadside exhausted?

8. Prepare revision guidance individually

Recently I visited a school to discuss how to change the level of performance in Geography. I asked the subject leader what he was doing. He said that for the first time the school had bought revision guides for the students. *But did they use them?* I asked him.

He didn't know. What a subject teacher determined to make big changes might do is prepare a single sided A4 revision sheet on each yellow topic in her subject and attach to it copies of all the GCSE questions on that topic over the last four years. This would be issued to the student, following an intensive revision session with the teacher and the student would be required to attempt the questions within a week and hand them back for marking. It is specific targeted work on the yellow areas that makes the difference.

These are some of the strategies shown on the hypothetical plan. Teachers will add to them, modify some and ignore others but those who mean to make the difference need to know where to apply their effort to maximum effect. They have to share their plan with their subject leader, not only for approval and agreement but so that together they can agree actions they both support and believe will succeed. Then, when it happens, they can both celebrate.

Action points

- List of borderline students issued to class teachers
- Action plan drawn up by teachers to deal with these students separately
- Checks made on level of coursework and plans in place to reach B- or C+
- Teacher discusses strengths and weaknesses with each borderline student using a personalised learning check list
- Special classes introduced for groups of four on specific topics known to be below C grade
- Second examination in which the student has a good chance of reaching C grade planned
- Agreement on what support the school wants from parents

Chapter 12

Through revision

The difference between what we are doing and what we're capable of doing would solve most of the world's problems
Mahatma Ghandi

Revision is a key activity. Most students know this but a surprising number do not know how to revise. For many students *revise* is an odd word. I use the word *re-visit* when talking to students. Re-visiting is going back to some place you have been before. You can re-visit old haunts. You can go by car or bus or walk. But too often there are too many other things to do that are more attractive than re-visiting, whichever way you choose. Increasingly these days schools organise study skills days for year 11 so they can pick up ideas on how to revisit old school work. These can give you good ideas on why it is advantageous to re-visit but can also suggest ways of making it more interesting. Last year I organised two revision days for different groups of students. A team of study skills experts was hired to teach at both days. The first group, all A* and A students, rated it as helpful and inspiring. The second group were borderline students. They were restless and detached from it all. They were bored and uninspired yet the content was much the same. We did not repeat the exercise for the borderline students this past year. Study skills days in schools need to be carefully analysed. The difficulty may be because mixed ability groups are looking at the same issue. Several schools are abandoning whole year groups training in study skills simply because so many middle grade students do not tune in to the important lessons about revision. Borderline students need training in revision and encouragement to engage in it in smaller groups.

Young people know they should revise and many intend to. Yet great numbers of them don't. Schools, for their part, want them to revise and have devised various means to help them. Foremost amongst them is the preparation of a study programme, with a succession of dates with spaces beside them. Meetings are arranged, often using tutors, for the spaces to be filled with subjects that the student will revise. Students like to prepare these. They complete them, decorate them and take them home. They feel good and the school feels it has done its bit.

For borderline students a more sophisticated approach will be needed. David Smith is the hypothetical borderline student shown earlier. The school holds data about him shown in figure 11 on page 78.

What subjects should David revise? Below is a plan of action about revision.

How to create your own success – a step by step plan of action for David, with asides for teachers

1. Consider all the subjects you do.

2. Classify them as Green (probably will get C or higher), Yellow (maybe will get C) or Red (Definitely won't get C)

Student	Form			Prior Attainment
David Smith	11ZA			455
Subject	Present	Predicted	Potential	Teacher
Maths	E	D	C	Mrs Wilson
English	D	C	C	Mr Keith
Literature	D	D	C	Mr Keith
Science	DD	DD	CC	Miss Alam
History	C	B	B	Ms Hyatt
French	E	D	D	Mme Charaud
ICT	CC	BB	BB	Miss Dover
Design Graphics	E	D	D	Mr Frazer
Total	3	4	8	

figure 11

Aside 1 – In David's case
the green subjects are English and ICT
the yellow subjects are Maths, Literature and Science
the red subjects are French and Design Graphics

3.   Check these classifications with a teacher.
Students can make wrong judgements about their potential but teachers can also deceive students by building false hope through inflated assessments. There needs to be honesty.
Taking all green and yellow, work out which are revisable and list them.
The implication here is that green and yellow matter more than red. And they do! At least they do in the context of achieving 5 A* to C grades. They do not matter more as subjects nor should the red subjects be ignored in lesson time but if students are going to dedicate their own time to revision it needs to be with optimal effect.

Date	I hour session	1 hour session
18 March	English	ICT
19 March	Maths	Literature
20 March	Science Biology	Science Chemistry
21 March	Science Physics	English
22 March	ICT	Maths
23 March	Literature	Science Biology
24 March	Science Chemistry	Science Physics
25 March	English	ICT
26 March	Maths	Literature

figure 12

Aside 2 – So David lists

 English
 ICT
 Maths
 English Literature
 Science – Biology, Physics and Chemistry

4. Put two of these on each day for the next four weeks, a total of 56 slots, with your teacher's help.

Aside 3 – The programme for David is shown in figure 12 for a sample covering just nine days

This programme presupposes that you are going to revise for two hours each day on the dates shown. You have the power of veto. You may decide on any day that you are not going to revise but your revision supporter wants you to make that decision in advance and leave that day blank. Once it is agreed and committed to paper your supporter wants you to make a commitment to do it. You will make the commitment alright but will you do the revision?

Aside 4 – Alternative approaches

An alternative approach invites the student to agree how much revision time is needed for each subject being studied. This approach means that allowance can be made for subjects where revision takes a different form from others (for example Art and Mathematics may require a quite different method). It means also that all subjects will be revised, not simply the yellow and green, with differentiation being proportionate rather than not revising red subjects at all. Some teachers are more comfortable with this.

Some schools introduce a bonus plan. This is a reward system based on revision undertaken above and beyond that which was agreed. It is surprising how often this is attractive to students given that they had no previous record of volunteering for extra work! Once students have achieved an agreed level of work, many find the bonus incentive an encouragement to do yet more. Once this begins to happen the teacher may reasonably assume some problems have been cracked.

5. Give your supporter a copy of your programme
Once the programme is complete you keep your copy and give one to your revision supporter who helped you to prepare it.

Aside 5 – This person must be someone who has a good relationship with David

It should be someone he likes to please and from whom he will take advice. It may be his team leader from the motivational scheme.

6. Arrange to meet your supporter one week from now and each week thereafter

Aside 6 – Principles

The problem with all revision programmes is that students like to prepare them but they find them difficult to keep to. How can the teacher help with that? Understanding these principles may provide a clue:

- People do things if they know someone is **interested** in whether they do it or not

- People do things if they know that someone is going to **check** whether they have done it or not

- People do things if there is some **reward** for doing it, intrinsic or extrinsic

Most revision schemes drawn up in a school show interest in a student to the extent that they help her to prepare it but that is where it stops. There is often no formal checking system in place to assess whether the student has engaged with the programme. This seems to me the biggest mistake. I admit to making it myself for far too long. The good intentions of the student do not deliver and no one knows it. On the basis that human activity is energised by 'What's in it for me?' considering some tangible reward might be an idea.

So the proposal is to arrange a weekly scheduled meeting with each student, organised and led by the student's revision supporter.

Here's a typical conversation:

Your schedule says that on Tuesday you would revise History. What did you do?

What might the student say? *I didn't do it.*

You hope not but it is as well to know. Response should be disappointment rather than annoyance. You emphasise the partnership and say you are doing your bit and you thought there was an agreement that he would do his.

My experience is that when interest and support like this are agreed, the answer is different. The student will tell you what he did. It may be done well but more likely it won't be because he has poor study skills. He didn't listen when he should, remember? Now you can teach him one-to-one how to revise well.

So he says, *I read my notes.*

Good, you respond, *did you highlight your notes? Did you use mind maps or spider diagrams or extract the key words or use post-it notes?* You know all the ideas that he does not know but now he sees the relevance and is ready to learn. It is a personalised approach to study skills. You pick one or two subjects to discuss but he can't guess which you will choose.

These meetings need twenty minutes every week, preferably during school time. Where can the teacher find the time? One way is to try to match the supporter's non-contact time with the times the student is being taught a red subject. If the teacher of a red subject will allow the student to miss twenty minutes to see you, this can work wonders. But some are reluctant to do it. The subject teacher may object that she does not

want the student to miss that lesson. You can point out that some of that same teacher's students are missing other people's lessons to increase their chances in her subject. It is give and take – there are potential benefits for all.

7. If you have done really well your supporter may tell your headteacher and your parents

Aside 7 – Rewards
Reward is important. It has to be tangible and it has to be desirable. The supporter can say that he will tell the headteacher how well David is doing and ask her to send for David to say, *Brilliant, David, well done. Keep it up.* This takes no time at all and is significant reward and recognition for unseen effort and has strong motivational effect on students who are unaccustomed to such personal interest and encouragement.

The supporter may send a note home, without telling David, saying much the same thing as the headteacher.

You can give other rewards: vouchers, tokens or even cash.

8. You should ask your subject teachers what is the best way to revise your chosen subjects

Aside 8 – Embarrassment
Borderline students are afraid to ask questions. Often they lack confidence or self-esteem. They are embarrassed lest they seem stupid and don't like letting on. They feel it and they don't like to display it. The subject teacher ought to have a vested interest in this student anyway because he is on her list too! There should be coherence between what the supporter is doing and what the subject teacher is doing.

9. You should find out from the teacher which bits of those subjects are the ones where you need to get stronger

Aside 9 – Personalising learning for students

Consolidation is important. Revising topics that the student can already do has value but not nearly as much value as finding out which areas are weak (yellow), obtaining a revision sheet and GCSE questions, and trying to change yellow to green. The supporter can help the student to do that, in some cases representing the student to the subject teacher to find out.

10. You should ask the teachers if they would mark those GCSE questions and show you how to improve

Aside 10 – Diagnostic marking and self-esteem

The subject teacher may forget how important the marking and correcting of this work is. Yellow becomes green when the student knows what to do to make it change. Analytical marking with scheduled time to review the work carefully needs to be built into the revision. The benefits to a student's confidence are huge when yellow turns to green and he knows why.

Practical problems with revision

Some assumptions are made when teachers ask students to revise. First, that they know how to revise and what to revise and this is often not the case. But another problem is:

Where will students revise?

It is thoughtless to assume that all the borderline students have a suitable place to prepare for GCSE. What are the criteria for a suitable space?

1. It needs to be quiet

Ideally it should be a place where a student can think and concentrate, without siblings running in and out. Some students have several siblings, some share a bedroom and some have no separate private place to work. This complicates revision enormously and in some cases makes it almost impossible.

2. It needs to be free from interruptions

During a residential conference for borderline boys time was given to discuss problems with revision. One boy said honestly, 'I want to revise and I mean to, but when my mates ring on my mobile and ask me to go out I am just not strong enough to say no.' There is no hope when his girl friend rings. The phone interrupts and so does the television and computer. For well-motivated people these seem mere excuses but for borderline students it is a critical issue.

So what can be done? For the enthusiastic and committed people living in cramped or difficult conditions places need to be provided which are conducive to study. The boy who admitted his ready distraction asked the headteacher: 'Can we have a room at school, supervised by staff for two hours after school so that I can do all my work then and afterwards put all my books away? Then, for the rest of the evening, I can do what I like without feeling bad.'

3. The school may wish to introduce incentives for borderline students

Ideas like this meet with a mixed response in the education profession. 'It shouldn't be necessary,' say some. True, and for many middle aged, well-qualified people it wasn't necessary. But some young people need all the motivation that can legitimately be provided. One school allowed students to claim £1 per after-school session as long as they attended at least 15 out of the 20 sessions offered. That is not a bad deal for both the student and the school! Because boys respond to short-term targets, any such scheme needs to be provided over a limited period of say 20 sessions and then begun again. Boys do not respond well to open-ended targets or start but don't follow through.

If a school is going to do this, call it something attractive. 'The Homework Club' has no great appeal. We called ours 'The Night Club'. Somehow it sounded better when sixteen year-old boys shouted to their mate on the corridor, 'I'm off to the Night Club'.

A school in Manchester struck a deal with a curry house which had a room upstairs. Students would stay for two hours working upstairs, after which the curry would arrive. They called it 'Curry on studying'. Jamie Oliver may not find the idea attractive but it clearly had a lot of appeal.

Good revision can add half a grade to a GCSE performance but it has to be good and it has to be done. Borderline students often don't know how to revise effectively. These ideas might help you to help them.

Action points

- Decide how to structure study skills days

- Identify which subjects a student needs to revise

- Plan a revision programme for each individual

- Appoint revision supporters

- Arrange times when supporters can meet students in school time

- Set up a Night Club for those without good revision spaces at home

- Consider a reward system for attendance

Chapter 13

Through planning

You can't cross a sea by merely staring at the water
Rabindranath Tagore (1913)

To reach the destination of a substantial increase of GCSE grades at C or higher requires an action schedule, not just wishing it, although desire is fundamental. During the Wimbledon 2005 final, a supporter of Roger Federer waved a banner proclaiming: '*Federer is Betterer*'.

And on that day he was. It was interesting in the light of such a superlative performance to hear him declare next day that he wants to improve certain aspects of his game. That ambition is likely to keep him at the top for years to come. Wanting to be better does not mean that you aren't good.

Alongside desire there has to be *hard work*. Substantial change takes a year to make its first impact. *If people knew how hard I had to work to gain my mastery, it would not seem so wonderful at all*, said Michaelangelo. Popular author Stephen King observed that *Talent is cheaper than table salt. What separates the talented individual from the successful one is a lot of hard work.*

Most school leaders seem to have great aspiration and are prepared to work hard but success also requires detailed and rigorous planning. An ancient proverb says *if you fail to plan, plan to fail*. A plan is needed because so many people are involved, considerable resources are being spent, the project extends over a whole year and there is so much at stake. Developing and implementing a plan is crucial to success. Some schools design a wonderful plan but do not follow through on its implementation. At the time of euphoria on winning the Olympic Games bid for 2012 much was made of the outstanding planning of the committee led by Sebastian Coe. Here was a determined man working with a dedicated team. His father said of Coe that *he is the most competitive person I ever met*. Determination is vital for success. A competitive spirit can be helpful too.

There are clear stages to plan for:

1. Prepare the ground

Part of the initial work on London's Olympic bid was to counter any doubts that London wanted to host the Olympics. It was far from unanimous and much persuasion was needed. That ground was well prepared. Had it not been, the bid would surely have failed.

The leadership team in any school seeking large scale change has to create *dissatisfaction* with the *status quo*.

Jacobs (1994) devised the mathematical expression about change:

$$P = A * B * C > X$$

where P is the probability of making a change successfully (see chapter 1)

A is dissatisfaction with the *status quo*

B is a clearly desirable end state

C is an identified and specific series of steps on the way to that end state

X is the perceived cost involved in making the change.

Hawkins (2005) talked of the wisdom of the wise old fool Nasrudin. After a very long board meeting in which the board had strategically planned their management of change programme, they inquired of Nasrudin how long he thought it would take to turn the company round.

> *Well, it all depends,* Nasrudin began.
> *On what?* they asked.
> *On how much you are enjoying the view from the way you are presently facing.*

The teachers in school may not feel dissatisfied with the *status quo.* They may quite like the view. Many in my school did not feel much dissatisfaction with the way things were at GCSE level. The school was doing well, it seemed. No one was urging the need for change. But full credit to most of them, they came to see that things could be much better, so became dissatisfied with the current situation. It is the job of the school leaders to create dissatisfaction. It is a delicate business because if handled badly it can lead to demoralisation. The secret is to persuade people that the school has done well but that by using new approaches it can do still better for its students. That is the *Federer focus.* Kotter (2002) went further, maintaining that without *a sense of urgency* change is likely to falter early on and that *by far the biggest mistake people make when trying to change organisations is to plunge ahead without establishing a high enough sense of urgency.*

Preparing the ground is crucial if the chances of success are to be high. A sense of urgency can be awakened by talking about how far you are behind what you believe is possible. The vision of an attractive, desirable new position will add to the urgency to get moving. If you can convince significant numbers of people that 10 per cent on your GCSE score is achievable some will say *let's get started!* The more vivid the attractive vision, the more likely you are to make change happen. Planning the detail is what Jacobs called itemising the steps on the way. Without these the chance of successful implementation of change is low.

2. Find the resources

Excellence in Cities funding offered great opportunity for those fortunate enough to qualify for it. The money was meant to be used in part at least to raise standards. Many schools have no such resources but feel the need to make changes. Money will have to be found. Though resources are tight, much depends on where you set priorities. It seems inconceivable that having established a sense of urgency you don't then find resources from somewhere to address the issues to make the vision happen.

Introducing some of the ideas in this book will cost money. Some estimates of expenditure are given in several subsections of the plan below. These deal with costs for people and allowances, time, rewards systems, student opportunities and training. Welch (2005) argues that people make three common mistakes when launching new initiatives:

- They don't flood start-up ventures with adequate resources, especially on the people front

- They make too little fanfare about the promise and importance of the new venture

- They limit the new venture's autonomy

It is not often that schools *flood* any venture, that's not the language of education. However, changing GCSE performance requires significant resources. Without them this change will have limited success. Penny pinching on raising standards is a mistake. I am amazed how easily schools can find money for ICT equipment which is important but seem reluctant to spend money on the *big aha.* The fanfare that Welch talks about begins during the preparing of the ground stage but makes itself heard fully at the launch of the plan. It is important to make something of the launch. Five minutes as part of a staff meeting won't do. The fanfare reflects the importance you give it. The big push to raise standards needs a big launch and that may cost money too. *We don't do this sort of thing in education,* some say, but increasingly schools are doing this sort of thing and you are going to have to if you don't want to make the mistakes Welch warns against.

3 Select the motivational team

You will need a plan for appointing people to this team. If you decide on a lead teacher will this be a deputy head with many other duties or will you appoint a specifically chosen person as this book advocates?

- When will this person be in post?
- What will be their role?
- How much time will they be allocated for this work?
- What allowance will they be paid?
- What will they be expected to achieve?

An appointment needs to be made as soon as possible in an academic year to affect results by the end of it. You can make it a one-year appointment with a basic allowance, say £2000, and a bonus of £1000 if the target is reached. You might prefer to pay an allowance without any bonus or you could decide to pay nothing at all but allow one day per week for this work, effectively costing the school around £6000. With the advent of Teaching and Learning Payments there is opportunity to organise your structure to include this post. Surely raising standards and teaching and learning are linked?

> Whoever is appointed will need time and time means money. This role alone is likely to require £5000-6000.
>
> The scheme will not succeed with a leader alone. There needs to be a team.
>
> Do you ask teachers to do this in their 'free time'?
>
> Do you use adults who are not teachers, because it's cheaper?
>
> Do you make a time allocation to teachers to do the work?
>
> Do you pay these teachers an allowance?
>
> Do you give teachers time off *in lieu*?

The teachers need time to work effectively and they need to meet regularly outside school time. The school leadership expects them to show dedication and commitment to the raising standards cause and to represent and uphold its importance in the staff room. This is serious work. Some schools have offered teachers one period per week for it, others have paid an honorarium of around £1000. Having six staff in position, this will cost £6-8000. Some schools struggling with this financial conundrum have opted instead to release teachers for two or three days after GCSE and A level is finished *in lieu of* time spent on the raising standards project.

4. Training and developing the team

Jim Collins (2002) talked about getting *the right people on the bus.* You selected the right people so now it is a case of training and developing them, honing their skills and securing their whole-hearted commitment. All this will need time allocated for being together, working through what they believe and what values they cherish. The group will need to decide on its policies and the practicalities of the systems they will use. They will need to consider the starting point and calculate the attractive end point to which they are heading. They will need to plan the steps on the way. Some teams spend a residential weekend together to thrash these matters out; others meet after school. It needs to be planned early in the academic year and have money allocated for it. Occasionally schools join with other teams with some experience to share ideas and this can be constructive. The cost is likely to exceed £1000, one way or another.

5. Consult and brief the subject leaders

There are two major strands to impacting on GCSE performance. The motivational team has been allocated time and now thought is needed about how to consult and brief subject leaders. Their involvement is crucial to success. School leaders need quality time with subject leaders too, to ask questions, listen to misgivings and to new ideas and to reach consensus on the practical interpretation of the plan. This is not going to be achieved by fitting discussion into regular meetings alongside departmental matters. Subject leaders might be paired up to develop ideas and to be critical friends to each other. This work is a teaching and learning responsibility so it fits well with the guidance for schools covering 2006 to 2009. Because proposed change is threatening for some people and can provoke negative responses, creating time for constructive discussion is essential.

6.   Fix the key points

Know where the key points are. In *Changing Towards Excellence* (2003) John likens the plan to a train timetable. If Kings Cross is the destination, the fixed points on the way from Newcastle are Darlington, York, Doncaster, Grantham, Peterborough. You have reached King's Cross when you hit a 10 per cent improvement in GCSE. Too many people intending to reach Kings Cross break down somewhere in between but are not quite sure where. The fixed points to build in to the annual planning schedule for the school's journey are:

a)   Identification of the borderline focus group.

The members of this group need to be finalised by October prior to summer examination the year after.

b)   Raising awareness of all students in year 11

Great care needs to be taken so that all students understand what the school will offer to each different group over the next year. Students receive ideas well if they are convinced that thought is being given to them all and that genuine differentiation of provision is being made on their behalf. Emphasise the different approach to the needs of the borderline group and why that is desirable in the context of moral purpose. However, at the same time, students need to be told of:

- the extensive provision being made to meet various kinds of special need

- the plans to provide extended opportunity for gifted and talented students

- the personalised planning to be offered to all other students

The more specific you are, the more convincing will be the message. Assemblies to communicate these matters need to be scheduled with care.

c)   Involvement of parents

Students participating in the borderline activities should do so voluntarily. Teachers know they need support, encouragement and help but the students need to realise this and opt into the scheme. If it is promoted well, this causes no problem as most people are attracted by something they recognise as beneficial and enjoyable. Some schools have individual photographs taken of the borderline students and send cards home to parents with the student's picture on the front and a personal hand-written message inside. This might read:

Dear Mr Ahmed,

I hope you like Khalid's photograph. We took it recently and send it to you now to let you know that I am working with Khalid to help him to do well in his GCSE next year. You know that he might do well, but he might not, and I want to work with him to give him the best chance of success. I will keep you up to date with how he is doing but for now I feel sure you will support me as I seek to make the most of his ability. It will be fun and I hope next summer I will be able to celebrate his success with him and you. I want to invite you to hear about what the school is planning at a meeting at school on 23 October at 7pm. I hope you can be there to support Khalid and the school.

Yours sincerely,

The system you are using should be explained to parents at a special meeting. It could begin with a video clip showing students receiving their examination results the previous year, backed by suitable music. Properly produced, this film can be very motivational. The meeting needs to be given a big promotional push to gain as much support as possible. Copies of a three minute video showing results day at a London school are available on the CD. Though this is not your school the images are powerful and can be used to stimulate and motivate students in other schools.

Be prepared for the problem of parents whose children are not on the scheme wanting them to be. This has always proved to be the most common difficulty.

d)   Residentials
One of the specific ideas that you might communicate will be that residential opportunities for different groups of year 11 students will be organised throughout the year. Typically, a programme would extend over one night or two and would feature:

- team building activity to raise self-esteem

- how to revise

- how the brain works

- study skills in action

- subject specific sessions

- planning a revision programme

- how to make the most of coursework

- leisure and fun activities

Specialist input to such residential events would be assigned in a way appropriate to each group. Our school found that mixed groups of gifted and talented students valued these events highly and that single sex groups were better for borderline students. When a programme is planned well in advance teachers are prepared to commit themselves to it. Many schools pay teachers for this extra involvement.

Residentials cost about £50-£70 per person per day, depending on location. The school will decide how to make these attractive to students. Sometimes schools pay a subsidy of up to 50 per cent of the cost and students

whose families cannot afford to pay go free. Including payment to teachers, this enterprise could cost as much as £8000. Local business and industry occasionally support such events. Fun activities are essential. Laughter and enjoyment create significant motivational momentum.

e)   Trial examinations and follow-up
Dates for trial examinations are in place in all schools and these need re-thinking. The following questions may prompt discussion:

- Are trial examinations taken seriously by most students?

- Do most students prepare for them?

- Do teachers adequately prepare students for them?

- Do students gain significant benefit from them?

- How well do trial examinations replicate the real thing?

- Are these trial examinations having as much benefit as they could?

Particular consideration needs to be given to the pros and cons of the existing system for borderline students. For them the trial examinations often:

- reinforce insecurity

- create demoralisation

- convince students that success is beyond reach

Another problem is the time spent in lessons afterwards going over the examination papers. It would be more effective if:

- borderline students had special preparatory revision sessions and if examination results were issued as they are in the 'real thing'

- support and advice was available soon after results are published.

In some London schools in 2005, results of trial examinations were issued in the hall on a scheduled day using the procedures that would be employed that summer. This was done to emphasise that the examinations should be taken seriously, the students experiencing the emotions of success or failure when the results were issued and receiving follow-up support, advice and challenge. Schools reported that this strategy had made a big impact on students, focused their minds in a new way and gave them a chance to change their attitude and behaviour with professional help. The teachers who ran this experiment intended to repeat it and made their plans accordingly.

f) Second trial examinations

The list of borderline students is modified throughout the year but particularly after trial examinations. Some students may be added who have potential to be a 5 A* to C student without yet achieving it. A considerable number of these borderline students will never have passed at C the examinations you need them to pass. This does not build confidence and puts pressure on students when they have never reached that level before. Some of the schools also experimented with a second trial examination, for borderline students only. This required careful planning by subject leaders. Administered wrongly it can lead to yet another 'failure' even nearer to the real examination. Those who trialled this successfully reported that they

- prepared the students for it in very small groups

- tried hard to create conditions for success

- celebrated successful outcomes to increase confidence

- de-briefed students fully on outcomes, focusing on those parts which could be improved still more.

Some problems were encountered. Subject leaders did not prepare properly, the tests were low priority and it was not easy to make time for these extra examinations. Schools thought these difficulties were surmountable and that the potential benefits were huge,

more than justifying the effort. Planning in advance reduces some of the obstacles.

g) Revision planning

Revision is often begun too late. This can be corrected by marking on the school calendar when programmes have to be in place. This is particularly important for borderline students for whom systematic, organised and supported revision can make a big difference. It can even be planned into residential events if they are well timed and if doing so will incur no extra cost.

7. Plan the detail

According to a fable, a family of mice was being pestered by a cat.

> *Let's go and see the owl*, said father mouse, *He'll give us advice.*
>
> *Easy*, said the owl, *Put a bell on the cat and you'll hear him approaching.*
>
> *But who'll put the bell on the cat?* asked the mouse.
>
> *Ah well*, said the owl, *I make policy, I don't bother with details.*

You will have to bother with the details. Several schools have started with enormous enthusiasm but falter long before the year is over because they gave insufficient attention to ensuring that the actions were planned in detail.

8. Build in the accountability

The way to ensure that things happen is to devise a clear plan, including scheduled accountability dates. These will need to be decided by the school's leaders and have two areas of focus. The motivational team will have considerable autonomy but will know that they will be expected to account for their actions and to report progress at monthly meetings with school leaders. This is likely to be welcomed by a newly appointed team charged with a huge responsibility. It will be much more challenging to introduce accountability systems into a group that formerly had none. If subject leaders are unaccustomed to being called to account they may be resistant. Six-weekly meetings between the headteacher or school leaders are essential, at which subject leaders can report how plans are progressing with regard to the borderline students. Little cost is involved in this process, except in headteacher time and in creating time for people involved in initiatives to have meetings. However, when these activities have borne fruit you will want to celebrate, so set aside money for lavish celebration with all staff. Is 10 per cent on GCSE worth £2000, say?

9. Create the right conditions

You have worked hard all year. Your teachers and support staff have invested hours of time and committed enormous energy to your vision. Now is the time to put it all to the test. It's examination time. And what often happens?

- Students are put into a large space that is unattractive, too cold or too hot, sometimes badly lit

- They are addressed every session by a person who frightens them to death, who tells them there may be a man from the examination board behind the hall curtains to catch those who cheat

- They enter the examination room not knowing where they will sit or who will be next to them

- They will be sitting for two hours in a stifling environment and be dehydrated by the second half of the examination

- The tension as they approach the examination is palpable and made worse by having to walk in total silence to their desk. The examinations officer insists on a deathly hush except for the sound of shuffling feet

- The supervisors resemble border guards, unsmiling and austere

This is an exaggerated scenario. No school will manifest all these alarming traits but many will manifest some. There are reasons for this. Schools do not want students to cheat and are accountable if they do. The examinations are in the hall or gym because that's the only space big enough. Its suitability is rarely questioned because there is no alternative. It is impossible to control the conditions easily.

All this is understandable but it is disastrous to have the students who have received so much attention feeling intimidated when it comes to the point of demonstrating what you have taught them. What can be done?

- Tell them in advance most of the rules that operate in the examination room so that little remains to be said

- Have a teacher skilled in encouragement telling the students before the big examinations when most students are present how good they are and how they are about to demonstrate it. The message should reassure, encourage, build confidence and get students ready to give it their all

- Have the students enter the hall to music. Devise ways of making the environment as pleasant, non-threatening and inspiring as possible

- Allow the students to have a bottle of water on their desk. Science has taught us many things about dehydration in recent years and we should take heed. Physics notes are unlikely to be concealed underneath the bottle cap

- Encourage the supervisors to smile and look as though they want the best for the students. This does not imply that they will allow cheating. It means they care about the outcome and they want the students to do well

- Have a *brain gym* session before each examination, either in the examination room or elsewhere so the students don't spend the first ten minutes waking up or warming up

All this needs to be planned for. The devil is in the detail. You will have invested so much that you won't want it wrecked by forgetting to plan for the days when it is put to the test.

Earlier we considered Jacobs' equation. The probability of success depended on dissatisfaction with the *status quo*, having a clearly defined and attractive end point and some identified steps on the way. Jacobs added a 'greater than' symbol at the end. He believed that the outcome you sought had to be worth all the effort required to bring it about. X was 'the cost involved'. Some of the costs have been indicated.

Adding about 10 per cent to GCSE scores can be done. No doubt there will be some who say it can't. George Orwell received a rejection slip from a publisher considering his book *Animal Farm*. It said '*it is impossible to sell animal stories in the USA*'. He proved them hopelessly wrong. You too might be able to do what seems impossible. Plan for it and be ready to pay the cost involved and then expect the change to happen.

Action points

- Make your mind up to plan for success

- Establish dissatisfaction with the *status quo*, but be careful

- Find whatever money it takes to make the difference

- Have clear interim points at which progress will be systematically checked

- Plan the residentials

- Take a close look at the examination room

- Establish and implement a plan to improve examination conditions

Chapter 14

Through teaching and learning

*They know enough who learn
how to learn*

Henry Brooks Adams

Whatever else schools might be, they are primarily learning organisations. Firstly, they are places in which our young people are educated and, secondly, the institution itself has to be able to learn and adapt to change. Developments in our understanding of the way young people acquire learning have been dramatic in the last twenty years. Until the advent of GCSE, external examinations in the majority of subjects largely assessed the mastery of content through extended writing. Memory and literacy were paramount. Even success in the Sciences was dependent to some extent upon the commitment of formulae to memory. Modern languages examinations were almost wholly written. In the eighties the world demanded a different profile of a citizen and we were harnessed to a different beast. The ability to recall facts still remained essential, but understanding, communication other than in written form and skills has become recognised as far more important. Students adapted themselves to the demands of coursework, while teachers laboured over ever more complex mark schemes. Successful schools quickly recognised the need to adapt teaching to meet these demands and education became more relevant, accessible and enjoyable for a greater number of young people.

Society now perceives the need for another shift in emphasis. You are charged with the mission to develop lifelong learners with independent study skills, through the Holy Grail of Personalised Learning. There is a wealth of new and exciting research into the way people learn, and you have to devise ways to use that knowledge to develop learners capable of picking up new skills and assimilating different bodies of knowledge throughout their lives. Doubtless there will still be a unit of currency built into the assessment of young people as they leave schools, not dissimilar to the current 5+ A* to C standard, by which their ability to learn, and ours to teach, will be judged. This is going to demand another big change in the way you approach your craft and your colleagues will need your leadership to be clear and thoughtful throughout the process.

Whatever happens it will always remain true that gifted teachers can impart knowledge through caring relationships and that school leaders must support and sustain staff with this developing talent. However, as interest in and knowledge about learning grows you must challenge even your most gifted colleagues to reflect upon their core activity and develop their practice.

A common story

None of this is news to headteachers, although it is rarely possible for them to find time to reflect on it in any depth. It is clear from government announcements, conference speeches, the educational press and wider media comment that student understanding of learning is becoming an increasingly important feature of the future in schools. It is common now to refer to the senior leadership team in schools as leading learners, yet it is rare to meet a headteacher who has time to stay abreast of the many new developments in learning theory. Often it is a responsibility that is delegated to someone else in the organisation. A glance at job descriptions for assistant and deputy headteachers show that in recent years Raising Standards and Teaching and Learning feature prominently in the profiles of jobs being advertised.

Many people have considerable expertise in this area, and there is a reassuring wealth of knowledge about theory in the profession. Applicants for posts often impress an interviewing panel by referring to lists of academics and theories researching how students learn. It is impossible to go into sufficient depth in an interview to find out precisely where a Director of Teaching and Learning might take pedagogy in the school, but once in place the successful appointee forms a coalition of interested parties and begins to effect the first major development in practice on their list. They generate an initiative or two and invariably link up with a Local Authority consultant, who adds a few more essential ideas to the mix. They may also attend courses, which prompt a second wave of initiatives that both excite and exhaust the newly formed Teaching and Learning Team. In addition there are people in the organisation beavering away with the literacy and numeracy strategies, which have pedagogy as part of their remit. Special needs students, who often have the clearest understanding of the learning process, receive a distinct diet, and schools with *Excellence in Cities* funding have an identified gifted and talented coordinator delivering training on learning styles that, at its best, complements provision elsewhere. Something of this kind is happening in most schools, even though teaching and learning policies are not a central feature of school life. There is no well-established common approach to teaching and learning yet.

Theory of learning

Scholarship on the nature of learning has produced a number of approaches that can be taken to learning:

- de Bono's coloured hats
- Smith's Accelerated Learning,
- Kolb's Learning Cycle
- Assessment For Learning
- Gardner's Multiple Intelligences and
- Bloom's Taxonomy

The National Learning Strategy proposes a series of models for consideration, as do the National College for School Leadership and the training that underpins the *Excellence in Cities* initiative. All these models are founded upon sound propositions. They are rational, intelligent, sensible, and have articulate and committed advocates of their benefits. Any one can form the basis of a high quality, high return approach to student learning. However, the combination of several can be confusing, muddled and counter-productive. It is common in schools for some staff to employ one strategy, while others use another. Some teams of teachers create a synthesis that suits them best whilst others are allowed to throw their hands up in frustration and confusion without direction from school leaders and go back to the tried and trusted framework they have used for years. This creates further confusion in the mind of the young learners going from one learning model to the next throughout their school day. In this kind of environment the impact of learning theory is minimal and a firm understanding of the nature of a person's learning is left to chance.

A whole school plan

It is obvious that this approach cannot be the most effective, and school leaders are in a strong position to put matters right. Leaders are busy people with a burgeoning set of responsibilities as part of their role. They are required to micro-manage many aspects of life within their organisations. This entails policies on budgeting, bullying, equal opportunities, discipline, exclusions, pay and conditions, uniform and many more. All are important in running schools with clarity and fairness, but how can you conduct your business without the need to develop and apply a policy concerning your principal function? Clearly a strategic plan for teaching and learning should be an essential element of good school leadership.

Howard Gardner (1999) establishes the need for leaders to develop the narrative of their organisation; to tell the story of the struggle to achieve what is developing in the school and the challenges that lie ahead. The leader establishes the qualities the organisation has, the values it stands for and the tactics used to meet the demands placed upon it. For the story to stick it has to be simple enough for brief recitation, and repeated many times by the leader until it becomes an accepted part of *the way we do things round here*. In schools it is crucial that the leadership builds a narrative structure for learning that

colleagues can identify with and work through. The headteacher, as principal narrator, must communicate a vision for learning which teachers support and in which young people will be able to share and benefit. Does this happen in your school? How often is it seen as the most important feature of the daily routine?

The model

Any single framework can be adopted as a basis for a teaching and learning approach in a school, be it one of the existing models, a careful synthesis of two or three, or even one that you devise yourself. The important role for leadership is to determine what the framework is going to be, to apply it and keep all others out of the structure, at least during the period of implementation.

In 2001 I visited Canada as part of a team of teachers from the LEA that employed me at the time. I was keen to see how a nation which had not yet been through the reform process undergone by most western nations used freedom from a National Curriculum and regular standardised testing. I was particularly impressed by two schools, one of

---

de Bono's Six Coloured Hats (1999)

This theory identifies six different forms of thought and suggests that they need to be used in isolation by groups of people working and learning together. These are:

White – Information. What facts do we need to proceed with this?

Red – Emotion. How will people feel about this idea?

Black – Cautions. What are the problems that we face?

Green – Creativeness. What really amazing ideas can we come up with on this topic?

Yellow – Positivity. What are the benefits of a particular course of action?

Blue – Organisation. What have we achieved so far? Where do we go from here?

Using de Bono's approach young people become aware of what type of thought is being encouraged and what language to use to demonstrate successful thinking in this area. It requires a disciplined approach to the language and thinking employed at a given time in the learning process.

Gardner's Multiple Intelligences

This model is based upon the belief that our intelligence comprises at least seven different facets that vary from person to person. This suggests that different individuals will access learning through tasks that are designed to employ different aspects of intelligence such as:

Verbal linguistic

Logical Numerical

Musical

Visual Spatial

Kinaesthetic

Interpersonal

Intrapersonal

This requires teachers to give considerable thought to the structure of tasks set, which should lead to expression in the target intelligence. It is very intensive on resources and planning.

---

which served a community facing challenging circumstances. These schools were positive and successful learning environments. The children were actively engaged with the wider process of learning as well as the immediate task being undertaken. What ran through the schools from top to bottom was a language of learning that was common to all participants. One used de Bono's coloured hats as a basis and the other Gardner's Multiple Intelligences.

I am sure that these two schools demonstrated the other hallmarks of a vibrant and successful school: clear leadership, good continuing professional development practice, high expectations and a culture of celebration. But I have seen these operating in many places without the buzz of excitement about learning. What was truly inspirational was the shared commitment to a particular way of doing things that each school had itself decided upon and the way it was understood and learned by the whole school community.

Making an impact

The particular model you choose does not seem to matter. It need not be de Bono or Gardner. All models have their own strengths and weaknesses. Some are rather complex and some bring problems associated with being labelled. Others focus on a structure for lessons, while the emphasis for some is on tasks within the lessons themselves. There are significant resources and training implications implicit in this. **The crucial challenge for leaders is to commit the change agents within their school to a model they can believe in, and do everything possible to embed it into the culture of the school.** The benefits of introducing a clear model for learning that is common across the school are:

- you can evaluate the practice of colleagues with reference to a common approach
- teachers can share ideas across departments more easily

- students should be able to discuss their learning with staff across the curriculum with clarity and understanding
- there will be coherence and a shared sense of purpose
- communication across learning will be a standard feature of school life
- students and staff will both recognise that learning is paramount in your school
- all involved in the school will recognise they are part of a learning community

Were you to start from scratch and create your ideal school, would you implement the approach to learning you have now? If not, why continue to pursue it? The argument that things should remain as they are because that is how they have always been simply doesn't stand up. You should determine what the best approach to learning should be and establish it across the organisation. People who work and learn there will find the clarity of leadership on learning refreshing, empowering and inspirational.

One approach

I have focused on *Gardner's Multiple Intelligences* (1983) as a framework for language about learning. The process of introducing a new focus on learning included:

1. forming a group of staff to lead on its delivery

2. planning a CPD session for the whole staff

   This began with a plenary to explain the reasons for having such an exclusive focus, the idea behind the particular model and the different aspects of the approach. The lead teachers delivered a series of sessions on each of the intelligences in a carousel before teachers went into teams to look at the implications for their lesson planning. Activities were devised by teachers that would meet the needs of students, taking account of their different intelligences. Staff profiled their own range of intelligences.

3. delivering a similar session of training to all the students in the school, getting them to profile their relative strengths and weaknesses.

    This encouraged coherence across the school: staff and students in harmony on vision and purpose

4. inviting parents to an evening session that gave them a chance to see what was going on in school and how it affected their children. They also profiled themselves

5. disseminating information about student profiles for practical applications in classrooms

6. requiring teachers to refer to the Multiple Intelligence model in lesson planning and in each child's report to parents

The consequence of this focus is that talk about learning is common across the school. There is constant lively dialogue about learning between all the stakeholders in learning and learning has become a key part of planning.

Students will almost always need to demonstrate their learning through writing but they can now understand why they might find some aspects of school life easier than others. When each teacher delivers a lesson based on an understanding of multiple intelligence then at least they experience teaching that suits their strengths from time to time and can see that their interests are considered important.

It is important not to profile students through a fairly crude mechanism and assume they will only function in a particular area and never develop a different range of intelligences, but it does move towards a more individualised approach to learning styles that suits a greater number of young people.

There are a large number of variables in the success of a school in public examinations. It is not always obvious which cause has produced which effect. However this new emphasis on learning may well have been part of the significant improvement in examination performance that we have experienced. A 20 per cent improvement in GCSE performance over two years has many causes. Both a focus on borderline students and an emphasis on learning have played some part.

Action points

- Identify and agree a model for teaching and learning

- Find a team to deliver it

- Plan CPD for staff, students and parents

- Determine what structural evidence you need to show that the initiative is being employed in classrooms

- Plan activities to keep the model at the forefront of people's thinking

Chapter 15

Through dynamic leadership

Most of the change we think we see in life is due to the truth being in and out of favour
Robert Frost

Securing better examination grades for the students at the boundary, and for the school, is achievable. It will not happen if the experience of previous years is repeated. It will change if the students enjoy a different, better final year of study from those who have passed through school before. It is not sufficient to say we will just do more of the same and expect it to pay off. Your team needs to be led somewhere slightly different and to see this year as a particularly important one in the life of the school.

Believe in yourself

The leader of a school has the most crucial role within it. You are in a position to make a huge difference in the culture of your school and the lives of those who work and study there. Of course everybody in the organisation plays an important role but there is no hiding from the fact that the structure and direction of the organisation depend upon your leadership more than on any other single factor. You can effect massive improvements if you are inspired to. If you are not it is difficult to see how change that will have a big impact is possible. Your performance and demeanour are an important part in the well being of everyone in it, directly and indirectly. So if you are

hopeful, positive and energetic about your ability to shape the future, others will respond with enthusiasm. If you feel beleaguered by examination performance, inspection regimes, league tables, staffing shortages and all the other aspects of leadership that you cannot control, your school is going to feel as though it is getting through this stage in its history in the hope that things will feel better soon. They won't until you decide to challenge people to make the difference from within the organisation itself. To simply manage responses to shifts in the external environment is to make the difference someone else wants. Harris (2002) writes that *by definition good leaders are not only enthusiastic about their jobs and the potential and achievements of the organisation in which they work, they are also believers in their own judgement.* She is right to highlight the need to begin with yourself if you want to develop the confidence and involvement of others.

You should challenge yourself and ask if you are driven by the same moral purpose and principles you had when you were just a young teacher. Are you inspired by the same dreams of making a difference? There are young teachers in your school who need confidence and inspiration from you. Everyone in the school is able to do so much more good if they feel their leaders have a sense of purpose and a vision they can buy into.

Preparing yourself

To make the difference advocated in this book you need to think of hearts and minds and begin with yourself. What is the difference you want to make? Is it to add 10 per cent to the GCSE A*-C figure, or more than that? Do you want to improve outcomes for the more able students, whose performance may be the more vital indicator for your school? Be clear and specific about the target because if you are vague you are demonstrating a lack of commitment or confidence, both of which are crucial to the enterprise. Your conviction can mean so much.

The Athletics World Championships of 2005 were held in Helsinki. The favourite for the 100 metres was the American, Justin Gatlin, although there were a number of serious contenders and the commentators predicted a close race. They filmed the athletes in the waiting area preparing for the event in the final minutes, and it was noticeable that Gatlin sat quietly on his own, while others chatted or played up to the camera. On the track, as others warmed up, he walked the whole length of the track from the start of his race and stood on the finish line for a few seconds before walking back. In his head he had already run the race from start, through pick up to finish – and won. There were other influential factors; confidence, training, physiotherapy, prior record and current form but he visualised that win so intensely that he added sheer force of will to his other advantages. To be successful in any leadership role you must do the same. Imagine the early phases and how important it is to start the initiative right, know how it is going to feel in the most demanding periods of the transition from the current state to the more successful one you are working towards, and visualise the benefits that success will bring. If you can do this and believe in your ability to make this happen, the conviction will communicate itself to others. To suggest to others that this initiative might be a good idea and is worth attempting, even though it may not work, is to sit on the blocks while the winner prepares himself for victory.

1. **Why do you want to make this difference?** It is my preference to focus on the students but it is valid to think of the school in abstract terms as your principal interest because you are its primary custodian. A reason may be that you believe that each young person who gets over that 5 A* to C boundary will have choices they would not otherwise have had. This is bound to make a difference to many young lives. Every young person who is able to choose a course with a higher entry point creates a space on the course below for a student with less talent. Society functions best when the right people with the right level of appropriate skills find the role that suits them best. This is only possible if young people attain the results they are capable of. Enabling this is one of the biggest contributions you can make to society. Students should be able to leave you with a range of knowledge, skills and understanding that help them cope with life and make their own contribution. The quality of teaching in the vast majority of schools is now high. It would be a cruel waste of effort if we managed to develop these features in our young people but their qualifications did not reflect it. An approach needs to be adopted that helps teachers and pupils get the benefit of the years of hard work that predate preparation for terminal examinations.

2. **If your school achieves an improvement in results it will feel like a different place to work in**. Just as it is difficult to get out of a downward spiral, or break down a culture of coasting, success breeds success. It is possible to sustain year-on-year improvements for an extended period once you demonstrate that you have the means and the will to build a culture of school improvement. This is the most obvious way to do it.

3. **The most important factors in change within any organisation are the people within it.** As a leader you need to consider the impact on your own working life of the change you seek and then think hard about how other people will experience it. Fullan (2001) writes: *We have become so accustomed*

to the presence of change that we rarely stop to think what change really means... at a personal level. More important, we almost never stop to think what it means for others around us.

Believe in your students

As a leader you must have a view on the potential of the young people you serve. More than you intend to change systems you intend to change *them*. The structures you put in place are only there to make this happen.

- Is there a limit to what they can achieve and if so what is it?

- Is it based on objective fact or are you imposing it yourself?

- Do you believe that when you decide to make this difference the students are capable of responding positively?

Begin by looking at schools that deliver superb results for students from a similar community to yours. Don't look for possible reasons why it might be more difficult for your school, just look at the young people involved and ask yourself if your own students are not as capable and deserving. If they are, you already know you can match outstanding performance. It is almost certain that the other school is doing so well because it dared to try and achieve more than had been possible before. The potential resides in the young people, the daring lives in you.

It doesn't just happen

Young people are capable of so much if someone they respect believes in them. Self-belief does not simply appear in the hearts of the young: there are too many things in their lives that cause them to doubt themselves. For teenagers the default position is some form of angst about appearance, potential or personality. Confidence begins to grow when they have something upon which to base their self-worth. Many young people grow visibly when they are conscious that someone feels they are worthy. Your belief in the ability of your students communicates itself to them.

Students believe what teachers tell them. If experienced teachers tell them they will not achieve much, that will be the outcome. The message can be communicated explicitly and implicitly. Either way it is unacceptable. Your voice is the most influential. What you say about year 11 is crucial. If you allow them to be known as a bad year you are likely to pay for it. You can change things. Is there a significant proportion of your year 11 students who could leave your school with more choices and more confidence in life if you focus hard on their attainment? In important respects, students have their limits set by the adults around them and this is as true of expectations as it is of behaviour. Give them the signs and symbols that proclaim your belief in them and make that belief all-pervading. How can you do this?

- Tell them in assemblies that they have the capability

- Get their parents in and share the news with them that you know their children can do this

- Put the targets up in public spaces around school

- Let younger year groups know what the older ones are going for

- Ask students in the corridor if they are heading towards the goal you have shared with them

- Encourage staff to talk to them about your view of them as the special year group who will make the breakthrough

- Tell the story

- Let them know you will go the extra mile, or two, to ensure they succeed

Stories about students need to be told. To have most effect Kouzes and Posner (2003) recommend that:

- you know something about the students

- your audience can relate to your story

- the story you tell is vivid and detailed, though brief

- there is a sense of time and place adding reality to the story

- colourful and animated language be used

- you should recognise emotions speak so that contact is made with people who sense as much as they analyse.

Students are an immense source of such stories. Use them:

- to reinforce the vision

- to demonstrate transformation

- to empower the positive influences in the teaching staff

- to energise fringe players to encourage new commitment to the cause.

Try to be a presence in their school lives to an extent that is new to them. Make them feel positive and encouraged about their prospects. Visit their classes on a consistent and regular basis and make interactions as positive as possible. Withdraw students on such visits when you are told they are doing well and tell them how proud you are of them and what a difference they are making for themselves and the school. Where necessary withdraw students causing problems and tell them you are disappointed that they are letting themselves and the school down. Explain that you will be in other year 11 classes soon and you do not want to hear the bad news again. If you do, it is time to act!

According to Kouzes and Posner (2003) the first law of leadership is *if they don't believe in the messenger, they won't believe the message.* Epitomise your message by everyday actions, day in and day out.

When you launch the scheme to students, be open with them. Tell them what you want to achieve and why and explain to them the reason for prioritising the students you believe will benefit most from your attention.

Let them know that you understand how offering extra support might feel exclusive but make the case that looking after a group of people within a scheme has a positive effect on everyone around them. Teenagers have a strong sense of justice. If you explain that you believe that what you are doing is right and that you are doing it because you care, they will give you a fairer hearing than most adults. Even if they don't agree with you, they will accept that you feel it is right. There is something in it for them to be told that this important figure in the school community has confidence in their ability, wants to achieve something very special with them and is asking for their help. Believe that they will give your idea a chance and they will.

Believe in your team

Who will lead with you on this initiative? You are going to have to be closely involved but you cannot manage the whole thing yourself. It will provide an opportunity for you to demonstrate trust in those you feel have the capacity to act as change agents and a tremendous career development activity for some who have not had a chance to influence whole-school change before. Who will share your moral purpose and have the ability to see this through? Who might you be able to win over by involvement in such a key enterprise? Which aspect of the project appeals to which individuals: mentoring, teaching and learning, administration or communication? It is a wide-ranging activity that employs a number of skill sets that various people have.

It is wisest not to ask for volunteers, on grounds that everyone gets a chance to be involved in the contact with students. The skills you are looking for in this area are specialised. The people who lead have to be very good communicators, who can establish positive relationships that are focused on attainment. Some teachers are not great at standing in front of an audience and conveying the level of passion that generates enthusiasm among staff, parents and students. There are also teachers who seem unable to get alongside young people, especially those who are disaffected, and win their trust and affection. Other teachers form close enough relationships, but lack the ability to change the direction of students not eager to change.

There are two problems with asking for volunteers. The first is the fact that you are the headteacher and it is important and beneficial to secure your good opinion. This means some may volunteer to impress you, without necessarily sharing your commitment to the initiative. These teachers may not be able to devote the time and energy to the work when it begins to conflict with the priorities they consider important. The other problem is that teachers may not see their own strengths and weaknesses as you do. Your list of volunteers will contain a number of teachers who are unpopular with students who would not want to work closely with them over the course of their final year. The teachers concerned may well believe that this is exactly the sort of thing they are good at. It might appear to be an opportunity to confront these people over their perceived talents, but you may create bad feeling around the initiative or be tempted to include them and compromise the prospects of several key students. It is wisest to avoid confrontation of this type and at this time.

Although it is dangerous to surround yourself with people who share your own views and exclude those who challenge your ideas an enterprise like this, certainly in the first year, must be staffed by people who believe in it, in you, in the students and in their own ability to deliver it. And you must believe in them. They must be deployed in such a way that the right talent is matched to the right task and they will need to be supported. Here is a classic case of following Collins' (2001) maxim *get the right people on the bus*.

Believe in your teachers

Teachers are the people you must take with you on this venture. They must believe in your ability to take them through successfully. It is crucial to ensure that they are getting

what they need from you as their leader, and that you know what that is. This is the most vital feature of your leadership.

Mike Hughes delivers high quality professional development in schools. He is enthusiastic, realistic and provokes a high level of discussion. One of the most memorable features of a workshop I witnessed was a process through which he asked staff who they remembered as their most important teacher and why? Twice the outcome was the same: teaches listed enthusiasm, intelligence, patience, discipline and humour but easily top in both cases was that the teacher showed that she liked them and made them feel valued. Your own students would no doubt come up with the same answers. You might usefully ask yourself the same questions of those you lead and their views on leadership. They will not tell you that your most important attribute is your intelligence or knowledge. They will not suggest you are important because you manage budgets or determine salary levels, nor will they say they respect you because you have a track record as a successful teacher. Teachers appreciate leaders who respect their contribution and make them feel valued. You do not make the biggest impression on staff by getting them to see how talented and clever you are but by getting them to recognise these qualities in themselves. Everyone remembers some school leader in their career who made a point of letting them know that she believed in their potential.

How to bring about change

To bring about a significant change in the performance of students, it is wise to start by outlining how important everybody's contribution is to the project. You must demonstrate that attempting such a significant transformation is only possible because of the high skill-base that exists amongst the teachers and support staff. It is important to show that you are fully aware of how this work will impact upon teachers. Let them know that embarking on such a journey is exciting, frightening, challenging, intimidating and risky for you too, and that you need them to help you get through this as much as they need your support to come to terms with their own anxiety. You have to avoid creating a 'them and us' mindset. It is harder to think of a leader as uncaring, selfish, mechanistic and removed if she has stood up in public and shared her conviction that something marvellous is about to happen. However, people have to give up on the current comfortable position and face the anxiety that comes with a change of practice. People should know that it is as challenging and frightening for you as for anyone else. Telling teachers that you want them to help realise a dream that will lead to a big difference in the lives of many young people will encourage most of them to be involved with you at one level or another. Covey (2004) itemises six levels of commitment. These are:

1. Rebel or quit
2. Malicious obedience
3. Willing compliance
4. Cheerful cooperation
5. Heartfelt commitment
6. Creative excitement

Any commitment from 3 down is helpful. You will discover substantial commitment at level 4, 5 and 6 if you handle this wisely though, irritatingly, some will remain stubbornly resistant.

A key feature is establishing the moral case for your commitment. You believe this initiative will make a big difference and you feel that the potential exists within your staff. If you hold this view, it is not only right that you make this a priority, it becomes morally wrong to withhold this service from the students. It is your conviction that people should do what they believe to be right and the belief that this is ethically sound that drives you, not league tables, inspection regimes or any external *diktat*. Doing what is right does not always come easily but is always worthwhile. Colleagues will respect this. It is a difficult position to counter.

There will be people on your staff who have reservations about the project. Some predictable blockers will maintain their reputation of resisting most change. They will raise technical difficulties. Some will be people who want the best for the school just as much as you do but have genuine concerns that you will need to address. They will not have had as long to think this through as you and will take some time to be convinced. An advantage of detailed planning is the ability to construct answers to these queries in advance. Listen to them, show sympathy with their concerns and offer the persuasive counter-argument. To take any genuine challenge personally and railroad those who need time to think it through will lose their support and probably that of a few others. In any case, there may be considerable wisdom behind some aspects of this disquietude which if heeded could avoid problems later.

Believe in the parents

Make an effort to get the parents of the students involved into school and sell the idea to them with as much conviction as you can muster. Some may choose not to come, but many will attend. Go through the reasons for running a scheme such as this and outline the processes involved. Make it absolutely clear that the chosen students are not on the scheme because they are badly behaved or unintelligent. Otherwise parents will feel they are being criticised and will create a negative response to the process at home. The approaches you should take with parents are:

- You believe their daughters and sons have a lot of potential that you want to release

- you believe this idea will make a big difference to their final year in school

- you know about their approaches to study, homework and revision

- these very issues occur in many homes across the country every year and their children are entirely normal

- you explain the theory behind what you are doing and how it links to practice. Parents send their children into school in the hope that everything will go well for them every day. They get reports, invitations to parents evenings, newsletters and teachers contact them when things do not go well but some find it difficult to understand the level of care their child gets and the degree to which you understand them.

- you show that you have a clear understanding of their child, that you really want to help and that you understand how stressful it is for a parent to support someone through a stressful final year.

- you indicate how families can support the enterprise and encourage them to praise their children for their efforts early in the year

- you describe the family celebration planned for the last Thursday in August. Make it real, evoke the emotion, fire the imagination

- you stress your respect for them as important partners in these edeavours

This has to be a positive experience, reinforced by the presence of the headteacher, who clearly shares this vision.

Finding the time

The most difficult thing we have to manage in education is time. We could all do our job so much better if we had an extra day each week, or if someone else would do some of our more onerous tasks for us. This has been true throughout our career from classroom teacher to school leader. If you are setting up an improvement in GCSE results as your key focus for the year, you have to promise that you will try to stop anything deflecting from this. Whenever something comes up that might divert attention or take up valuable time, ask yourself whether ignoring it will do

any harm to the school or if the good it might do is worth damaging the prospects of excellent GCSE outcomes for your students this year. Local Authorities may want to deliver something to a particular category of teacher in your school, a government initiative might appear to warrant an audit of some form of provision, a request might come to support some form of extra-curricular enterprise involving teachers or someone might come up with an idea for tracking Performance Management, subject reviews, target-setting or any other number of worthy projects. Until you are sure that the capacity exists to meet these requests without compromising the focus on examination students, protect your staff from them and let them know you have done so.

'Finding' time implies that it is there but not being used to achieve maximum performance. Collins (2001) talked of top level leadership being marked by ruthlessness. The issue of determining priorities needs ruthless application.

The early phases

Before you approach students, staff and parents, ensure that all the logistical arrangements are in place. You will need to resource this programme for success. Where you spend your money flags up your priorities. Funding is an important way to signal your drive and determination. Teachers and parents do not sit and calculate the cost of activities such as this but they sense their high status from the flow of resources for them. The team has to be established, briefed and know exactly what will be expected of them throughout the year: to achieve this, the paperwork needs to be generated and a calendar of events drawn up. Those making the various presentations must be clear what is to be said and what the presentation is trying to achieve. You will need to schedule key points at which you intend to bring people together, check progress and offer encouragement. Even if the scheme is to be administered by someone else, it is important that you are seen to be aware how well it is going. And it is vital that you are recognised as being fully committed to it at every point.

Ensure that you are there at every stage in the launch: meetings between members of the team running it, staff discussions, parents' meetings, and meetings with the students involved. Watching someone repeat a similar presentation several times can be tedious and there is always something else we could be doing but it is the first time this audience has heard it and your presence will mean a lot to the speaker.

During the scheme

If the planning and administration of the scheme is done thoroughly, the launch will go well and there will be considerable momentum behind it for some time. Staff involved will look for positives and find them. A different set of relationships will build and the students will enjoy a sense of feeling special that will fuel their enthusiasm. Classroom teachers may well be pleased that youngsters who have been a problem in the past are making a greater effort. Keep the pot boiling by telling the story of the successful launch and the emerging transformation of some of the students. Tell them that teachers are saying what a difference it has made in their lessons. Give teachers the chance to tell the positive story too. Their voice is a significant influence and in this context better even than yours.

Mid initiative dip

At some stage in the process it will need reinvigoration. A teacher in the scheme may feel a little let down by trial examination results or the progress of one or two of their group. A department or less distinct group of teachers may decide that they are not happy with the way things are going and voice dissent, people may begin to lose focus and postpone meetings with students or not keep on top of the paperwork. Any number of things will crop up to make matters seem difficult. This is when you will be needed most. Some teachers on the scheme may need picking up and reminding that they

were chosen because you have confidence in them. Critics need to be heard – though it is unwise to give them a public platform. Their concerns need to be taken seriously. Commitment to the detail needs to be reaffirmed and any problems capable of solution must be dealt with. Significant change is never a walk in the park: there is nearly always a dark patch where things seem bleak, and doubt can creep in. This is when your positive, passionate commitment to this cause must be expressed.

Practical support

Attend events in the scheme to reinforce your interest. If there is a reward that involves a trip, go along and enjoy the company of the students and staff. If there is a residential activity, go and at least launch it, so everyone can see that it matters to you. Thank the participants publicly for their commitment. If you feel you could make it work, run a team of your own. Form a group of students and tell them you want to win because you are the head. It will become an integral part of the scheme, reinforce your commitment to it and make those involved feel very special. Apart from anything else, when the headteacher runs a team of students, other teachers want to beat her. Healthy competition is to be encouraged.

The outcome

If you lead with enthusiasm and commitment, this project will work. Plan a celebration for this and include yourself. When a positive set of results come in, leaders give themselves a pat on the back, often more from relief than joy, and almost immediately look for what might have gone better to inform practice next year. When you see the benefits of this project, take time to remember the risk you took at the outset and congratulate yourself on the number of young people who will enjoy opening their results envelope and taking them home to their families because you had the courage to lead on this. Take pleasure in making the difference you came into the profession to make. Inevitably you will want to congratulate the young people you have supported, as well as the teachers who worked on the scheme. Of course you will seek to build on this achievement and to manage your success to make this possible. The school will gain esteem in the community, the staff will enjoy a sense of collective achievement and be willing to support an extension of the approach, and the students in your school will enjoy being part of a place that is really going somewhere. On the first day back, remind the staff of the start of the journey and how you felt, thank them for supporting you and playing their part in the success and tell them what the next chapter of their story entails.

Exemplary leadership

Kouzes and Posner (2003) describe exemplary leadership. Exemplary leaders:

- model the way
- Inspire a shared vision
- challenge the process
- enable others to act
- encourage the heart

Exemplary does not mean charismatic. Leadership like this needs, rather, deep thought, careful planning and ruthless determination.

At a Catholic leaders' seminar I raised Collins' (2001) notion that top level leaders are 'ruthless'. A headteacher interrupted. *We don't do ruthless*, he said. But then ruthless in this context does not mean unfeeling. It is more about the resolve to be uncompromising in pursuit of the dream. For success with the *big aha*, Collins is right.

Action points

- Prepare your case and the counter arguments to it
- Ensure that you feel able to communicate enthusiasm and confidence in the project
- Identify the people who are most likely to make this work. Appoint them to lead it
- Sell the idea to staff and listen to criticism
- Involve parents at the launch
- Support every event associated with the scheme
- Involve yourself as much as possible
- Celebrate the success personally and collectively
- Be ruthless with yourself and in your priorities in school.

Chapter 16

Is it worth it?

The whole idea is to bring a smile to a child's face
Walt Disney

There were other spin-offs no doubt but Disney's moral purpose couldn't be clearer. In the context of examination results, bringing a smile to a student's face is a great motivation, certainly enough to make all the effort worth it.

Is it worth it? You will think it is when:

- you receive the results in the last week of August and analyse them

Most of you will enjoy a holiday in summer but find yourself becoming anxious as examination results' day approaches. So much rests on these results. One of your teachers will download the results from the website and have them ready when you arrive at school the day before issue. You glance quickly through and form a first impression. You ask the teacher what she thinks of what has been achieved. You spend half the morning scrutinising the individual scores while someone calculates the overall number of students with 5 A* to C. The examination analyst suggests cautiously that it looks like a good year. You can barely contain yourself.

> *We have broken 70 per cent and gone up this year by 12 per cent, but it's only tentative*, someone claims.
>
> *How sure are we?* you ask.
>
> *Pretty sure, but don't quote me yet.*

It's a good feeling. You wait a little longer for confirmation and while away the time going through your list of students one by one. Occasionally you skip a few to search for one you remember being on the borderline list. You decide to find them all and note how many achieved 5 or more A* to C. You count up that 18 of the 25 borderliners have made it. *Fantastic*, you say to yourself before heading back to see if the tentative results are now confirmed.

You know you have twenty four hours to wait before you tell anybody. It seems like forever. You want to share but that's for another day. Tomorrow!

- you share the results with students

You have not slept much and when you did you dreamed about results' day. Now it has arrived. You can see students milling around outside waiting for your declared opening time. Teachers have begun to gather and you smile and say, *It's looking OK*. Understatement, of course, but you have decided that everyone should celebrate at once. You order the doors to be opened. No one moves and then the first brave souls sneak to the results' tables. A deathly hush falls. It is the prelude to mayhem. Jumping, leaping and celebrating break out. Girls squeal. Some cry with relief and joy. Boys punch the air and swagger back to friends and tell them they have failed – only to laugh and reveal they passed 8. Mobile phones emerge from pockets. Sweaty trembling hands ... more squeals, more joy and more congratulations as parents share the delight.

All the while the Media Studies department is recording the scene. It is a day too memorable to miss. Students hug teachers. Teachers hug students. Everywhere there is jubilation. Nearly everywhere – not quite all made it. Some students know it could have been them but they had too many grades at D. They know why. Too late now though. They sneak away from the scene.

Tonight it's party time. You hear students making plans. It's celebration time for year 11. You leave them to their moment and retreat to share the joy with teachers in the staffroom, busy analysing their students' results. You console some but celebrate with many more. Close analysis will follow but for now it's pure joy. Is it worth it? Don't ask on that day. It may take too long to tell you.

■ you hear from students

Next day is a day off. You have drained enough nervous energy to last a life time but next week is different. There are letters from parents.

> *We know she could not have done it without the school. Please pass on our appreciation to all her teachers.*

> *Please say thanks to Mr Walton. Andy says it's all down to his encouragement.*

Students call to tell you they have a place at a local college because of their results. Your sixth form is expanding fast on the back of student achievement. Students have more choices, more opportunity and more confidence in their future. They think it's worth it.

■ you start the new term

You decided in July that this September would be different so you asked the Media department to film on results' day. You take an hour before the new term starts to view the film. You can hardly wait for the teachers to arrive for the new term. They see the screen at the front and imagine the usual analysis of examination performance by the deputy head. Instead, after your warm welcome, you introduce the film. It's only three minutes long but you cannot recall teachers being so attentive for years. Some actually cry as they see the unbounded delight of young people who had been in their class. They know they were part of the reason for the joy. You remember: the whole idea is to bring a smile to a child's face. It feels good.

When it is over, the teachers clap spontaneously. They clap themselves. They clap each other. A tear comes to your eye too. You thank them all. You tell them they should

"Well, I do have this recurring dream that one day I might see some results."

be proud of themselves. Then you tell them a story or two. You spent last week finding out which students supposedly with no chance had achieved a miracle. You tell them where these students started and you tell them where they finished. You tell them that they, the teachers, made it happen and they are fantastic.

This is no dream. We have seen it happen just like this. We have seen it in our own schools, we have seen it in other schools and we hope you see it in yours. Is it worth all the work? Silly question.

- you outline the vision for the new school year

For once, it is easy. People want to hear. They seem prepared to believe.

You say, *We've done it once. We know how we did it. We can do it again. What is more, we have learned from last year and will make some changes this year that will make it even better.*

You outline the ideas, you ask for thoughts over the next week or two on how teachers think the project could be better still. You capitalise on the momentum. You hope the feeling never fades. You promise yourself you will do all you can to stop it fading.

- you report to governors

You don't normally send results out in advance but this is too good to keep to yourself. Writing the letter is easy: just the right tone, not boastful but very happy. You outline the facts with little comment. You wonder if any will bother to call you. Some do. They are overwhelmed.

> *Please pass on our congratulations to all the staff.*

You pin the letters in a place of prominence on the staffroom notice board next to the letter from the Director of Education. He rang on exam results' day and said, *Well done. What you are doing for these kids is fantastic.* That felt good. You can't wait for the governors' meeting – and that makes a welcome change.

You decide that a couple of heads of department will be invited to the next governors' meeting. They haven't been before but their nervousness is tempered with pride and joy as they speak about their results. Governors say how pleased they are and ask that their gratitude is conveyed to teachers. You ask the teachers to tell all the staff at the next meeting. The newspaper called.

> *What was the secret?* they ask.

> *We have excellent staff and fine students,* you say.

There's much more to it than that, but the sound bite will do. Everybody feels good again.

Is it worth it? It feels more worth it every day.

- you see the league tables

You usually try to avoid looking but strangely this year you are waiting for them. The newspaper rings again.

Next day there is a letter from the Department for Education. You wonder, is it a notification of an inspection? But it isn't, it's an invitation to meet the Minister of State who has noted the vast improvement in your school. You tell the teachers that they ought to go because they did most of the work but that is not possible.

> *Do you want me to accept the invitation?* you ask them.

> *Yes!* they say. *Do it for us and tell us about it.*

Is it worth it? Ask Nick Ware at The Priory, ask Jim Rogers at Eston Park. Next year it could be you.

De Bono, in Tactics: The Art and Science of Success, *says the one thing that characterised successful people was this overwhelming desire to make things happen.* It is not about dreaming, except to formulate the vision, but about ruthless determination to succeed. And, all the while, like Disney, you know *the whole idea is to bring a smile to a child's face.*

Is it worth it? The smile alone is, but you'll get far more than a smile.

References

Some of the world's greatest feats have been accomplished by those not smart enough to know they were impossible
Doug Lawson

Barth R. (2001) *Learning by heart*, San Francisco: Jossey-Bass

Biggs J.B. and Moore P.J. (1993) *The Process of Learning*, Prentice Hall

Bohm D. (1996) *On Dialogue*, Routledge

Bossidy L and Charan R. (2002) *Execution: The Discipline of Getting Things Done*, Random House

Canfield J. (2005) *The Success Principles*, Element

Collins J. (2001) *Good to Great*, Random House

Covey S. (2004) *The 8th Habit*, Simon and Schuster

de Bono E. (2005) *The Six Value Medals*, Vermilion

de Bono E. (1999) *Six Thinking Hats*, Penguin

Denny R. (2004) *Motivate to Win*, Kogan Page

Dourado P. and Blackburn P. (2005) *Seven Secrets of Inspired Leaders*, Capstone

Earl L. and Katz S. (2002) *Leading Schools in a Data Rich World*, Kluwer

Fink D. (2003) *It's About Learning*, Routledge Falmer

Fullan M. (2001) *The New meaning of Educational Change*, Teachers College Press

Gardner H. (1983) *Frames of Mind: The Theory of Multiple Intelligences*, Basic Books

Gardner H, (1999) *Intelligence Reframed*, Basic Books

Guiliani R. (2002) *Guiliani*, Little Brown

Hargreaves D. (2003) *Education Epidemic*, Demos

Harris A. (2002) *School Improvement*, Routledge Farmer

Hawkins P. (2005) *The Wise Fool's Guide to Leadership*, O Books

Jacobs R. (1994) *Real Time Strategic Change*, Berrett-Koehler

Katzenbach J R. and Smith D K. (1986) *The Wisdom of Teams*, Harvard Business Review Press

Kotter J. (2002) *The Heart of Change*, HBS Press

Kouzes J.M.and Posner B.Z. (2003) *The Leadership Challenge*, Jossey-Bass

Nanus B. (1992) *Visionary Leadership*, Jossey-Bass

Owen J. (2005) *How to Lead*, Prentice Hall

Rowling J. (2002) *Heading Towards Excellence*, Trentham Books

Rowling J. (2003) *Changing Towards Excellence*, Trentham Books

Senge P. (1990) *The Fifth Discipline: the Art and Practice of the Learning Organisation*, Doubleday

Singer P. (1979) *Practical Ethics*, Cambridge University Press

Stoll L., Fink D. and Earl L. (2003) *It's about Learning*, Routledge Farmer

Welch J. (2001) *Jack*, Headline

Welch J. (2005) *Winning*, Harper Collins

Creating Success in Year 11
A booklet for students Spring/Summer 2006
Schedule of Monitoring 2006

Phase One	Meeting One	Meeting Two	Meeting Three
Team 1	20 Jan period 2	3 Feb period 3	4 March period 4
Team 3	20 Jan period 2	3 Feb period 3	4 March period 4
Team 4	20 Jan period 2	3 Feb period 3	4 March period 4
Team 5	20 Jan period 2	3 Feb period 3	4 March period 4

Phase Two	Meeting One	Meeting Two	Meeting Three
Team 1	24 March period 5	21 April period 6	5 May period 1
Team 2	24 March period 5	21 April period 6	5 May period 1
Team 3	24 March period 5	21 April period 6	5 May period 1
Team 4	24 March period 5	21 April period 6	5 May period 1
Team 5	24 March period 5	21 April period 6	5 May period 1

Subject report pages

for Student's name…………………………………… Team……………

Subject: Mathematics   Teacher's name:…………………………………..

Meeting Time	-3	-2	-1	0	+1	+2	+3
20 Jan							
3 Feb							
4 Mar							
24 Mar							
21 Apr							
5 May							

Subject: English   Teacher's name:…………………………………..

Meeting Time	-3	-2	-1	0	+1	+2	+3
20 Jan							
3 Feb							
4 Mar							
24 Mar							
21 Apr							
5 May							

Subject: Biology   Teacher's name…………………………………..

Meeting Time	-3	-2	-1	0	+1	+2	+3
20 Jan							
3 Feb							
4 Mar							
24 Mar							
21 Apr							
5 May							

Subject: Chemistry   Teacher's name:…………………………………..

Meeting Time	-3	-2	-1	0	+1	+2	+3
20 Jan							
3 Feb							
4 Mar							
24 Mar							
21 Apr							
5 May							

Subject: Physics   Teacher's name:…………………………………..

Meeting Time	-3	-2	-1	0	+1	+2	+3
20 Jan							
3 Feb							
4 Mar							
24 Mar							
21 Apr							
5 May							

Subject: Option A   Teacher's name:..

Meeting Time	-3	-2	-1	0	+1	+2	+3
20 Jan							
3 Feb							
4 Mar							
24 Mar							
21 Apr							
5 May							

Subject: Option B   Teacher's name:..

Meeting Time	-3	-2	-1	0	+1	+2	+3
20 Jan							
3 Feb							
4 Mar							
24 Mar							
21 Apr							
5 May							

Subject: Option C   Teacher's name:..

Meeting Time	-3	-2	-1	0	+1	+2	+3
20 Jan							
3 Feb							
4 Mar							
24 Mar							
21 Apr							
5 May							

Subject: Option D   Teacher's name:..

Meeting Time	-3	-2	-1	0	+1	+2	+3
20 Jan							
3 Feb							
4 Mar							
24 Mar							
21 Apr							
5 May							

Subject: Religious Studies   Teacher's name:..

Meeting Time	-3	-2	-1	0	+1	+2	+3
20 Jan							
3 Feb							
4 Mar							
24 Mar							
21 Apr							
5 May							

Subject: Physical Education   Teacher's name:……………………………………..

Meeting Time	-3	-2	-1	0	+1	+2	+3
20 Jan							
3 Feb							
4 Mar							
24 Mar							
21 Apr							
5 May							

Subject: To be added   Teacher's name:……………………………………

Meeting Time	-3	-2	-1	0	+1	+2	+3
20 Jan							
3 Feb							
4 Mar							
24 Mar							
21 Apr							
5 May							

Subject: To be added   Teacher's name:……………………………………

Meeting Time	-3	-2	-1	0	+1	+2	+3
20 Jan							
3 Feb							
4 Mar							
24 Mar							
21 Apr							
5 May							

Subject: To be added   Teacher's name:……………………………………

Meeting Time	-3	-2	-1	0	+1	+2	+3
20 Jan							
3 Feb							
4 Mar							
24 Mar							
21 Apr							
5 May							

Phase score sheets

Phase one scores for…………………………………… Team name:……………………

Subject	First score	Second score	Third score	Phase 1 total
Mathematics				
English (*2)				
Biology				
Chemistry				
Physics				
Option A				
Option B				
Option C				
Option D				
Religious Studies				
Physical Education				
Other subject				
Organisation				
Total				

Phase two scores for……………………………………..Team name:………………………

Subject	First score	Second score	Third score	Phase 1 total
Mathematics				
English (*2)				
Biology				
Chemistry				
Physics				
Option A				
Option B				
Option C				
Option D				
Religious Studies				
Physical Education				
Other subject				
Organisation				
Total				

Phase one Group Monitoring Form

Team:...............................

Subject	Student 1	Student 2	Student 3	Student 4	Student 5	Total
Mathematics						
English (*2)						
Biology						
Chemistry						
Physics						
Option A						
Option B						
Option C						
Option D						
RS						
PE						
Organisation						
Total						

Phase two Group Monitoring Form   Team:................................

Subject	Student 1	Student 2	Student 3	Student 4	Student 5	Total
Mathematics						
English (*2)						
Biology						
Chemistry						
Physics						
Option A						
Option B						
Option C						
Option D						
RS						
PE						
Organisation						
Total						

Phase one League Table

Team	Score 1	Place 1	Score 2	Place 2	Score 3	Place 3	Total Score	Final Place
Team 1								
Team 2								
Team 3								
Team 4								
Team 5								

Phase two League Table

Team	Score 1	Place 1	Score 2	Place 2	Score 3	Place 3	Total Score	Final Place
Team 1								
Team 2								
Team 3								
Team 4								
Team 5								

J R Rowling
Changing Towards Excellence Ltd

Appendix B

Identification System 2006-7

1. Assembling the data

Notes: Prior – data assembled from KS3 or Fisher Family Trust
Current – staff assessment as the student is now (maybe mock results)
Potential – professional assessment of what the student is capable of

Student	Form	Subject	Prior	Current	Potential	Subject	Prior	Current	Potential	Subject	Prior	Current	Potential	Subject	Prior	Current	Potential	Subject	Prior	Current	Potential	Subject	Prior	Current	Potential	Subject	Prior	Current	Potential	Subject	Prior	Current	Potential	Total of Potential C+
Will D	11Z	Ma	E	E	D	En	D	E	D	Li	D	D	C	RS	D	C	C	*2 Sc	D	D	C	Hi	D	E	D	Dr	D	C	C	Art	C	C	B	5
Teacher		JR				AK				AK				HN				SD				NL				DS				JH				
Salim M	11Q	Ma	D	D	C	En	D	D	C	Li	D	D	C	RS	F	F	E	Sc	D	D	C	Gg	D	D	C	PE	D	D	C	DT	E	D	D	6
Teacher		AJ				MS				MS				DL				HC				PB				MF				PR				
Amy C	11P	Ma	D	C	C	En	E	C	C	Li	E	E	D	RS	D	D	D	Sc	D	D	C	Hi	E	D	C	IT	D	E	D	BS	D	C	C	6
Teacher		JR				SV				SV				DL				SD				NL				MF				JB				

119

Identification System 2006-7

2. Using the data to identify borderliners

Notes: Prior – data assembled from KS3 or Fisher Family Trust
Current – staff assessment as the student is now (maybe mock results)
Potential – professional assessment of what the student is capable of

Student	Form	Subject	Prior	Current	Potential	Subject	Prior	Current	Potential	Subject	Prior	Current	Potential	Subject	Prior	Current	Potential	Subject	Prior	Current	Potential	Subject	Prior	Current	Potential	Subject	Prior	Current	Potential	Subject	Prior	Current	Potential	Total of Potential C+
Will D	11Z	Ma	E	E		En	E	E		Li	D	D	C	RS	D	C	C	Sc *2	D	D	C	Hi	D	E	B	Dr	D	C	C	Art	C	C	B	5
Teacher		JR				AK				AK				HN				SD				NL				DS				JH				
Salim M	11Q	Ma	D	D	C	En	D	D	C	Li	D	D	C	RS	F	C	C	Sc	D	F	E	Gg	D	D	C	PE	D	D	C	DT	E	D	D	6
Teacher		AJ				MS				MS				DL				HC				PB				MF				PR				
Amy C	11P	Ma	D	C	C	En	D	C	C	Li	E	E	D	RS	E	D	D	Sc	D	D	D	Hi	E	D	C	IT	D	C	D	BS	D	C	C	6
Teacher		JR				SV				SV				DL				SD				NL				MF				JB				

[ ] indicates SECURE and likely to achieve at least C

[ ] indicates BORDERLINE but may achieve C

[ ] indicates NO LIKELIHOOD of achieving C

Will has 4 secure and 2 borderline with 3 no likelihood - this offers a GOOD CHANCE of 5 A* to C
Salim has 1 secure and 6 borderline with 2 no likelihood – this offers a FAIR CHANCE of 5A* to C
Amy has 3 secure and 2 borderline with 2 no likelihood - it will be DIFFICULT to achieve 5A* to C

Appendix C

Personalised Learning Check list

Key: * understands ? does not understand

Student	Decimals	Fractions	Percentages	Area / Volume	Substitution	Equations	Simultaneous Equations	Vectors	Angles of Triangle	Parallel Lines	Cumulative Frequency Curves
Sean Adams	*	*	?	*	*	*	?	?	*	*	?
Allam Hussain	*	*	*	?	*	?	?	*	*	?	
Selina Mercer	?	?	?	*	*	*	*	?	*	*	
George Boatean	*	*	*	*	?	?	?	?	*	*	*
Zac Benjamin	?	?	*		*	*	?	*	*	*	?
Anita Parris	?	?	*	?	?	?	*		*	*	*
Will Bartram	*	?	?	?	*		*		*	*	?
Naseem Khan	*	*	?		*	*	?	?	*	*	
Ursula Young	*	*	*	*	*	*	*	?	*	*	?

What might you be able to tell knowing this?
1. Detect who is most vulnerable? e.g. GB
2. Group together students with a common problem SM, ZB, AP
3. Recognise where almost all students have a problem e.g. Vectors

What might you do knowing this?
1. Arrange small group teaching on specifics
2. Run after school classes on group problems
3. Hold lead lessons on key topics
4. Prepare banks of focused GCSE questions
5. Hold a second trial exam around these key themes once revision has been undertaken

Key Marginal Student - Amended Timetable

Student: Shaeed Mandir
It is anticipated Shaeed will get
English, English Literature, Opt A, Option B – that is 4 subjects at grade C or higher
It is believed he *could* get Mathematics and Science (2) – that is 3 subjects at grade C or higher
It is predicted that he will not achieve C in Option C, Option D and Religious Studies
Shaeed's best hope is to achieve 7 subjects

Shaeed's present timetable

Day /Period	1	2	3	4	5	6
Monday	Eng	Math	Opt A	Opt B	PE	PE
Tuesday	Opt C	Opt C	RS	Math	Sc	Sc
Wednesday	Opt A	Opt A	Eng	Opt D	RS	Opt B
Thursday	Math	Opt C	Sc	Sc	Opt B	Eng
Friday	Sc	Sc	Opt D	Opt D	Eng	Math

Shaeed's amended timetable – model 1
Option C taken out and replaced by Math (1 period) and Science (2 periods)
This model would mean dropping Opt C from his examination schedule

Day /Period	1	2	3	4	5	6
Monday	Eng	Math	Opt A	Opt B	PE	PE
Tuesday	Opt C/ Math	Opt C/ Sc	RS	Math	Sc	Sc
Wednesday	Opt A	Opt A	Eng	Opt D	RS	Opt B
Thursday	Math	Opt C/ Sc	Sc	Sc	Opt B	Eng
Friday	Sc	Sc	Opt D	Opt D	Eng	Math

Shaeed's amended timetable – model 2
One period taken from each red allowing Math (1 period) and Science (2 periods)
This model allows all subjects still to be retained

Day /Period	1	2	3	4	5	6
Monday	Eng	Math	Opt A	Opt B	PE	PE
Tuesday	Opt C	Opt C/ Sc	RS / Sc	Math	Sc	Sc
Wednesday	Opt A	Opt A	Eng	Opt D/ Math	RS	Opt B
Thursday	Math	Opt C	Sc	Sc	Opt B	Eng
Friday	Sc	Sc	Opt D	Opt D	Eng	Math

Model 2 offers more flexibility because it allows a choice of which lessons to take from Opt C for example. This is helpful when you want to put students removed from Opt C into a lower school class studying Science – at least there are three slots on the timetable when this might be the case. If it proves not to be the case then you might see whether Maths lower school classes fit in any of these spaces.

Appendix E

Rules of engagement for Key Marginals using an amended timetable

1. Students withdrawn from classes where they have no chance of grade C to do support work in subjects where they could get C should go into a lower school class studying the same subject that the student is trying to improve. For example, if Shaeed needs reinforcement in Mathematics he should go to a lower school mathematics class

2. The students has a spare desk in the receiving class and is contracted to fulfil these conditions:

   a) he arrives on time

   b) he works on work he has brought without any intervention from the class teacher of the receiving class

   c) he remains on task doing his designated subject throughout the lesson

   d) he makes his work available for inspection by the teacher at the end of the lesson

   e) the teacher signs a card indicating that he has abided by the agreement

   f) the teacher hands the card to the programme coordinator

In any one week Shaeed may have 3 cards reporting on how he has abided by the agreement made with him

3. If this programme is run for 25 key marginals, say, the programme coordinator should receive 75 cards, 3 for each. Results of these should be recorded and graded by the co-ordinator's team (on a scale of 1 to 4 say) so that the quality of responses of students to the support programme can be quantified. These should be transformed into the average score per lesson so that should there be a student with more than three cards in any week the system may still be used.

4. Two or three prize winners should receive rewards in the presence of the whole group

5. The co-ordinator might make clear to all 25 what qualities are being looked for in order to reinforce the importance of the programme

6. A typical score card might look like this:

Student present ☐

Student on task without supervision ☐

Student produced good work ☐

Student arrived on time ☐

If the teacher scores 1 in each box then clearly the student has a score of 4 to be recorded along with others. These will then be averaged prior to a formal judgement being made about winners.

It may help you...

to have a CD with the proformas shown in the appendix. These can be used as templates for documents you can use in your own school. They can be revised and amended to suit your local situation. Some schools have found the Creating Success Booklet particularly useful as they set up their own motivational scheme.

For further details about this CD, e-mail therowlings@hotmail.com.